Individuals in the Social Lifeworld:

A Social Philosophy of Heidegger's Dasein

Douglas Giles

Insert Philosophy
Praha

ISBN: 978-1-7358808-0-8

Insert Philosophy
Italská 209/17
Praha 120 00
Czech Republic

Contents

Introduction

How people interact with their fellow human beings is a significant philosophical question for philosophies of epistemology, mind, language, ethics, and politics. In this book, I will use several key concepts in Martin Heidegger's Being and Time to craft a theory of human intersubjective relations and individuals' social identity. Heidegger's concepts and terminology are idiosyncratic and at times opaque and off-putting, but I argue that some of them can be understood as connecting with areas of philosophy not frequently associated with Heidegger—specifically, ethical, social, and political philosophy.

"Dasein" is Heidegger's term for the distinct entity that humans are. Heidegger portrays Dasein as an inherently social being that responds to its environment in a pre-theoretical manner. Because Dasein is present in a social world—Being-in-the-world—Dasein is a way of life that is shared among members of a community. This conception is helpful in acknowledging that we live in our interrelations with others, and, further, understanding who one is as an individual is a relation of being with others. Embedded in a shared public world, individuals are constituted by other people, including much of the contents of their own minds.

But being formed by the world is only half of the story of Dasein. Heidegger says that care (*Sorge*) is the Being of Dasein. People are not only acted on by the world, but they are also involved in it, acting in the world on the basis of their concerns (*Besorgen*). The social world and the individual person are codetermined, meaning that individuals are influenced by the people around them and that individuals influence the people around them. Social groups are composed of their individual members. The social world is a public, shared world to which individual people contribute.

We need to incorporate both sides of this dynamic—the social world affecting the person and the person affecting the social world—into our view of intersubjective relations. We then can apply this view to questions of epistemology, mind, language, ethics, and politics. Heidegger's concept of Dasein is strong on the point that people are affected by the social world but is problematically vague on the experiences of individual people and vaguer still on how individuals respond to and affect their world. Incorporating subjective experience into Heidegger's conception of Dasein's Being-in-the-world will give us a more encompassing picture of how people interact and contribute to the workings of society.

If we understand Dasein as Being-there, then how do we understand the different, individual experiences of Being-in-the-world? We can craft from Heidegger's Being and Time an account of how Dasein exists and acts in the midst of social contexts if we take a different direction than Heidegger did. The elements are present in the early sections of Being and Time, but Heidegger decides to develop other ideas both later in Being and Time and later in his career.

The crux of my conception combines two of Heidegger's insights—that Dasein's knowing is a mode of Being and that Dasein brings entities close into significance and places them into regions. The insight into Dasein discussed in this book is that bringing close into significance extends to Dasein's knowing, which reveals the concept of Being-sphere—the mode of Being that differentiates each individual Dasein in its involvements and possibilities in its everyday Being-in-the-world. I have no eagerness for neologisms, but "Being-sphere" is my term for a new combination of several of Heidegger's points that will yield a clearer and deeper view of Dasein. This book describes the ontological structure of Being-sphere through a phenomenological analysis of how Dasein appropriates experiences and social norms into its differentiated and individuated experience of the world. Being-sphere enables a fuller explanation than Heidegger supplied of how individual Dasein responds in the face of das Man and other Dasein and how Dasein is individuated in the social lifeworld, thereby providing a foundation for answering questions of interpersonal relations and social and political theory.

The Conceptual Building Blocks

Dasein as Mineness and Being-in-the-world

Heidegger's concept of Dasein is difficult to define but it is central to his philosophy. The German word "Dasein" literally means "Being-there" and for Heidegger it expresses his ontology of the individual person as a being who exists in a world and understandingly and deliberately directs his or her self toward what he or she cares about in his or her world. The term "Dasein" is not equivalent to "person" or "self," because it means not a factual entity but the way a person exists—a person exists as a Dasein. Heidegger repeatedly uses the impersonal "it" rather than "he" and/or "she" when referring to Dasein, an odd convention that nevertheless has been adopted by commentators because it is in keeping with how "Dasein" is not equivalent to "person." How "Dasein" relates to "person" is debated by commentators. This incomplete definition of Dasein will be fleshed out by considering perhaps the two most important parts of Dasein—Dasein's "mineness" and Dasein's "Being-in-the-world," We will look at each in turn with the understanding that they are both equally fundamental and mutually interdependent grounding of our Heideggerian social theory.

The first thing that Heidegger tells us in his analysis of Dasein is that its Being is "in each case mine." (41) [1] As a Dasein, a human being, my Being belongs exclusively to me, and I am responsible for my Being and the choices I make about what concerns me and what actions I take. I am consciously and deliberately aware that my every experience, awareness, decision, and action is in each case mine, they are all traits of me and of no one else. In this way, my existence as a Dasein is characterized by my "mineness." We can understand this mineness as a self-owned locus of accountability.[2] Dasein owns what it is and what it does in response to what it can be. Heidegger stresses that Dasein understands itself in terms of the possibility of various ways of being and decides to which of its possibilities it shall pursue. (12, 41-44, 53) This is different from the existence of an inanimate object such as a tree, which has no

---

[1] References to Heidegger's *Being and Time* will be listed parenthetically as the original German page numbers. Quotations will be from the Macquarrie and Robinson translation. Heidegger, Martin. *Being and Time*. Macquarrie, John and Robinson, Edward (tr.), New York, Harper & Row, 1962.
[2] Haugeland (1982), 24.

awareness of its world or self and cannot have understanding or make decisions. Mineness is fundamental to Dasein's Being. The modes of Dasein's Being, such as what Heidegger calls "authenticity" and "inauthenticity," are grounded in the fact that any Dasein whatsoever is characterized by its mineness. (43) What a person can be, what he or she perceives and understands, how he or she behaves and what he or she expresses, all stem from that person's mineness. How an individual perceives his or her self and his or her place in the world is the center of that individual's world. This concept of mineness—Dasein as locus of its Being—is foundational for our later analysis of how a person comes to understand him or her self and the world around them.

Just as in each case Dasein is characterized by its mineness, in each case it is also characterized as Being-in-the-world. (53-54) My Being dwells in a world and my thoughts, choices, and actions are as much directed toward that world as they are toward my self. I am conscious that I am in a world and that my every experience, awareness, decision, and action occur within that world. My existence as a Dasein is characterized by my Being-in-the-world. It is *my* environment but at the same time I am immersed in and part of that environment.

Heidegger rejects a view of knowledge common to much of Western philosophy that a person peers out from a camera obscura-like mind at a world of objects. Heidegger rejects the ideas that knowing is simply a relation between subject and object and that knowledge can be arrived at through introspection or reflection. (59-62)[3] Such a view of knowledge is based upon the assumption of the self as an isolated subject and, as Heidegger points out, has the problem of explaining how an isolated subject can make its way out of its inner sphere into another sphere to know objects in the outside world. (60, 96-97) Heidegger says to the contrary, when I know something about the world, I do not leave my inner sphere and return to my "cabinet of consciousness" with the booty of knowledge I have grasped. I am always out there amidst the objects and my knowing anything, even my knowing my self, is grounded in my Being-in-the-world, my dwelling in and being a part of that world. (62) Knowing, in a Heideggerian philosophy, is similar to the philosophies of Dewey and Wittgenstein.

Being-in-the-world is an essential feature of Dasein's distinctive way of being. If we attempted to view the world as the collection of objective entities in existence, we would not reach the phenomenon of the world that people inhabit.

---

[3] See also Guignon's discussions of Heidegger's views on knowledge (1983 and 1984).

Heidegger is not suggesting that there is no objective world aside from human perception but argues that the world is known to a person in their Being-in-the-world; even an objective view of entities presupposes our Being-in-the-world. (64) The world is that in which I find myself and the world is that wherein all of my actions make sense. As we shall see, this existential fact is crucial in understanding human interaction and social identity.

Much of the secondary analysis of Heidegger's concept of mineness centers on what we could call the self-interpretive existentiality of Dasein. For example, William Blattner says that a "central existentialist thesis lies at the heart of Heidegger's conception of a human being." A person, he says, understands his or her self as "self-interpretive ability-characteristics," for example, being a leader or being an American.[4] Blattner is correct in that a person does engage in self-interpreting his or her abilities; this is characteristic of Dasein's mineness. However, Blattner is overstating the case in arguing that "Dasein is only its self-interpretive characteristics" and is "essentially self-understanding."[5] Heidegger believes that a person's capability to understand or interpret him or herself is not entirely self-interpreted and that Dasein is not just self-understanding. Equally fundamental and mutually interdependent with Dasein's own self-interpretive concerns are the influences on Dasein from other people, both individuals and society. (113-130) Blattner and similar commentators do not ignore the role of the world in Dasein's understanding of its possibilities, but their analyses could benefit from a greater emphasis on the worldly influences on Dasein.

To Blattner's observation of Dasein's self-understanding we can add John Haugeland's observation that "Dasein is neither people nor their being, but rather a way of life shared by the members of some community"[6] and Dreyfus's description of "human beings going about their business in a meaningful social world."[7] An understanding of Heidegger's thought must balance the self-interpretive mineness of Dasein with its dwelling within the world. A person's mineness and Being-in-the-world are the equiprimordial[8] grounding of how that

---

[4] William Blattner, "Existence and Self-Understanding in *Being and Time*," 178, 180-181.
[5] Blattner, 181, 182.
[6] John Haugeland, Reading Brandom Reading Heidegger," (2005), 423.
[7] Dreyfus, *Being-in-the-world*, 147.
[8] "Equiprimordial" is the translation of Macquarrie and Robinson for Heidegger's neologism *gleichursprünglich*. I take it to mean "equally fundamental and mutually

person takes on a definite character. (53) A person does not exist isolated from his or her environment (Heidegger uses the German "Umwelt," literally "the world around us") and a person is to an extent defined by their dealings with their environment.

We now to turn to the nature of these dealings. First, we will outline how a person's mineness contributes to their dealings with their environment through Heidegger's concepts of involvements, significance, regions, and de-severance. Then we will turn to how a person's involvements with other people influences their dealings with their environment through Heidegger's concept of Others.

Involvements and Significance

We are not passive perceivers of the world. We perceive and act within a world by understanding and interpreting it and making it our world. (148-149) Understanding is not strictly rational but both a projection of our self and an engaged seeing of the world. (150) A person's understanding of his or her world is structured by his or her mineness—his or her understanding, experiences, choices, and concerns. Our interaction with the environment is made manifest to us through our "dealings" in the world and with entities within-the-world. (66) Such dealings are made manifest through our ways of concern—what we care about—which is "the Being of a possible way of Being-in-the-world." (57)

Heidegger explains that we do not encounter mere "things" but "things invested with value." (68) Our world is filled with entities (objects), but mostly we interact with what he calls "equipment," also referred to as entities "ready-to-hand." Equipment are objects that we make use of for our daily needs. We understand equipment by the meaning we assign to them in terms of what we care about. Equipment ready-to-hand Heidegger defines as "essentially something in-order-to..." (68) In other words, we use a hammer to pound a nail, to repair something and the hammer is transformed from an more object into a piece of equipment by this assigning of a task in terms of our involvements. By involvements, Heidegger means how a person understands and uses equipment for his or her purposes—our in-order-tos, or the broader goals and possibilities for the sake of which a person acts. The hammer, in Heidegger's example of the work-world, (69-70) is a piece of equipment that was designed, built, and is now

interdependent."

possessed and used to fulfill the task of pounding nails. We understand a hammer as something used to pound nails, to fix a shoe, belonging to the cobbler, who uses it to satisfy his customers, that currently lies on a table, in a workshop, and so on. (70) Entities are used by a person for-the-sake-of-which— there is human purpose behind what a person does. As a result, equipment and its use are understood not through a theoretical characterization as mere objects but through a person's concernful involvement, which we can understand as that person's dealings and purposes. (66-70)

Heidegger acknowledges that we can consider equipment abstractly— disregarding its Being as ready-to-hand within the assignment-context of human involvement. But, he says, in doing so we lose some of the vital reality of these entities that link them to people. (71) Heidegger explains the connection:

> Thus along with the work, we encounter not only entities ready-to-hand but also entities with Dasein's kind of Being—entities for which, in their concern, the product becomes ready-to-hand; and together with these we encounter the world in which wearers and users live, which is at the same time (our world). (71)

This means that the shoe, and the equipment and work activities that produce the shoe, are assigned a place and purpose within an interrelated system of human involvements, which points us to a shared public world. People's involvements in the public world are in response to the wider world: a covered platform is built in response to the weather, lighting is installed in response to the darkness, and all of the work-worlds people create.

The relational totality of Dasein's involvements Heidegger calls "significance"—which makes up the structure of Dasein's world. The Being of the world is the interrelated system of Dasein's involvements, so every entity in Dasein's world exists within this significance. (87) Dasein's familiar understanding of significance is the means by which Dasein encounters its environment and understands equipment and its possibilities. All human actions that we witness are "for the sake of"—actions performed to fulfill a purpose meaningful to the person who acts. Thus, much of what we experience points us to other Dasein, as we will discuss later.

What we can take from Heidegger's concept of significance is that significance constitutes Dasein's view of the world. The world, the context of equipment, and the worldly character of what is within-the-world can be lit up by Dasein—freed for involvement and understanding. (75, 83) People, acting in-order-to, assigns values to what they do and with what they interact and establishes relationships between objects and between humans and objects. (68) A basic mode of Dasein's Being is to understand and interpret itself and the world around it. (87-88, 142-143) This is not necessarily a theoretical understanding but a practical one structured by Dasein's involvements. All human actions have a significance that cannot be captured through strictly theoretical or biological terms. In its very Being, Dasein comports itself understandingly toward its Being, its possibilities, and its everyday activities and involvements. It is in the essential nature of being human that we try to understand ourselves and the world in which we find ourselves. The world and everything in it make sense to Dasein in terms of its role in Dasein's significance. This is the basic structure of knowing the world; now we turn to how a person moves toward understanding.

Regions and De-severance

Heidegger explains that "the world of everyday Dasein which is closest to it is the environment." (66) The entities perceived and used within the world are significant within their environment, which is proximally understood as a whole by Dasein. The connection between people and their environment is found in a Being toward the world that matters to a person. (106-107) Ontologically, the totality of involvements places entities within a sense of space that is not objective space but existential space.[9] Equipment does not float free but belongs in a place determined by Dasein's concernful dealings, and this existential space Heidegger calls a "region." (103) Regions are not merely mental structures—they are environments that contain equipment. Regions are not merely geographical meaning they are formed by objects. Regions are laid out by people with regard to possibilities of Being and are encountered by Dasein to be co-determined by the totality of involvements for which the ready-to-hand entities are freed. (103-104) For example, we arrange the furniture in our home with regard to the possibilities of its use to us. The region of our home is co-determined by our involvements with the furniture as ready-to-hand entities as they exist in their place. The individual objects in the room have their place within the

---

[9] Dreyfus, in *Being-in-the-world,* distinguishes "physical space" from "existential spatiality."

whole of the room as we conceive it. Regions are ontological structures co-determined by the totality of involvements and imbued by Dasein with meaning, understanding, and concern. Similarly, the work-world, of the cobbler for example, is a region for those who work in it or visit it.

Heidegger then speaks of how people interact with and perceive the world—the character of de-severance[10], a concept that is little discussed in many commentaries. De-severance is a kind of Being that Dasein has with regard to its Being-in-the-world that means "making the farness vanish." (105) It would seem that Heidegger considers entities to be ontologically remote until they are brought close by a person—made available for concern. Dasein, he says, is "essentially de-severant"—"in Dasein there lies an essential tendency towards closeness," procuring entities and placing them in a region for use. (105) The de-severance of remoteness is, of course, a matter of spatiality, but it is also a constitutive state of Dasein's Being—it is a way in which people constitute their world. Ortega observes that

> connected to de-severance, our ability to bring things close, is the way in which we actually find ourselves in the world...A pencil is in a box in a completely different way than you or I are in a room. While the pencil merely takes up space in the box, I am in this room as a professor, a researcher; this room is not merely four walls, a ceiling and a floor that can be measured, but the place wherein I can live and carry out my tasks, desires, and goals.[11]

Through de-severance we turn everyday space into our space—make it subjectively ours—and we become *in* the world in an intimate way. He states that:

> The circumspective de-severing of Dasein's everydayness reveals the Being-in-itself of the 'true world'—of that entity which Dasein, as something existing, is already [amidst]. (106, emphasis his)[12]

In other words, the real world for people is the subjective world they uncover through their de-severance, which reflects their involvements. They lay out

---

[10] Dreyfus has a point that the standard translation of Heidegger's *Entfernung*, "de-severence," is unnecessarily strange. But since his arguably superior alternative, "dis-stance," has not gained acceptance, I will, for the sake of clarity, use "de-severence."
[11] Ortega, 28.
[12] I am going with Dreyfus's translation of *Sein bei* as "amidst" rather than Macquarrie and Robinson's "alongside," agreeing with Dreyfus's rationale. Dreyfus, xi, 44; Macquarrie and Robinson, 80, fn. 3.

regions and place equipment within it, assigning values throughout, and this is the world in which they dwell.

What we see here is how de-severance is a movement made by Dasein. The de-severance of any entity or concept is a possibility for Dasein, but it does not happen without Dasein reaching out and procuring something. The significance of human action is that people act in order to bring things close. This act could be a physical manipulation or bringing something under concepts that construct an understanding for a person or a group. People grant meaning to things and other people and focus their Being on those things that are meaningful to them. A work-space is a region formed through de-severance, and we can conclude that this is a result of human will—a work-world we create. Heidegger reminds us, however, that though we are free to embrace our possibilities, those possibilities are not infinite: "existentiality is always determined by facticity." (192) The facts of what we encounter are not chosen, nor can we choose the social conventions that constrain appropriate actions available to us.

Involvement with Other Dasein

Our analysis has now arrived at the question of how Heidegger conceives human interaction and how we can use these concepts to shed light on larger questions. Obviously, de-severance and regions are related to human dealings with objects, but do they also relate to dealings with other people? Heidegger says that "as Being-in-the-world, Dasein maintains itself essentially in a de-severing." (108) Does he mean this only in terms of entities, or does it also apply to interacting with other people?

Heidegger gives us an example to indicate that the two topics are related when he references in §26—his section on Dasein-with of Others (117-125)—the work-world of the craftsman he mentions in §15, which we can now see foreshadowed his discussion of Dasein-with. In §15—his section on the Being of entities encountered in the environment (66-72)—he says that work is using equipment (a hammer) toward an assignment (to make a shoe) to the person who is to use it or wear it. In other words, we understand that equipment serves the concernful dealings of other people. (70) In §26, he returns to that thread, reminding us that the equipment used

13

at work is assigned to other people for whom the work is destined. But here he expands the notion of assignment to the environmental context of equipment. (117-119) Heidegger gives several examples—the field, which because it is kept up shows itself as belonging to someone, and the boat, which, even though it is strange to us, we still understand belongs to someone. The existence of these environments discloses them as being in a world that belongs to the Dasein of Others a world that is, at the same time, mine.

We come across a region when we enter one formed by another human being. (103) For example, if we enter a waiting room of a doctor's office, we have entered a region. We proximally understand its purpose and easily can ascertain for what purposes the various pieces of equipment in the room are intended. Even if the room we enter is empty of other people, we proximally understand that it is a room built by, designed for, and used by people. In such a situation, the region would seem to be missing the people who make it a room, and it would seem odd to us.

We understand the world as a world shared with Others—a world inhabited and shaped by other people. Other Dasein

> are like the very Dasein which frees them, in that they are there too, and there with it. So if one should want to identify the world in general with entities within-the-world, one should have to say that Dasein too is 'world.' (118, emphasis his)

Although Heidegger calls them "Others," it is not that they are encountered as alien beings. When we encounter Others, we encounter entities like ourselves. He calls them "Others" not in opposition to Dasein but in similarity—they could be said to be Others-like-us. We do not immediately experience the Others as being in opposition to the "I"—we encounter them as being like ourselves amidst a world of things that are unlike us. Encountering another person in the world of entities is like being in a foreign country, not understanding their language, and suddenly hearing our own language being spoken; those words are lit up and we immediately gravitate toward the connection we have with the person speaking our language because they are like us. In any landscape, the presence of another person would stand out to us immediately and would engender in us an immediate recognition of Being-there-too within-the-world. We naturally bring people close, as Heidegger explains in his example of the acquaintance met on the sidewalk (107) Though the sidewalk is literally underfoot, an acquaintance observed twenty paces away is less remote. "Circumspective concern," he says, "decides as to the closeness and farness of what is proximally ready-to-hand environmentally. Whatever this concern dwells alongside beforehand is what is closest, and this is what regulates our de-severances." (107-108)

Therefore, our being with other people is Dasein-with. Heidegger characterizes the encountering of Others as oriented by that Dasein which is in each case one's own—our mineness (154)—and we recognize that Others possess their own mineness like our own. We recognize that, like us, these Others are characterized by their Being-in-the-world, their involvements and significance, and that they form their own regions and bring equipment close to themselves. This means that we encounter persons not as things but as Dasein-with in the world. (156) Heidegger gives the example of seeing a person "standing around." (156) We consider this person very differently than how we consider a post standing in the same place. Our assumptions are that the post is simply standing there, but the person is standing there for a reason; even if their reason is unfocused, we attribute a motive. People and social interactions are understood not through a theoretical characterization but through human concernful involvement. (118)

In the Midst of Others

We encounter people as participants in the world of our concerns, so our encounters with them are always understood in regard to our concerns. But Being-with means that our concerns relate to Others and their concerns. We are Dasein-with sharing the totality of useful equipment. Heidegger's examples of the tended field, the tailored clothes, the book from a store, and the discovered boat all speak to ways in which we interact and share the world with Others. (117-118) His examples show that the Others need not be actually present to us in order for us to interact with them. Being-with is true even when no one else is present. In the examples of the field and the boat, the owners of those entities need not be anywhere around for us to understand that they exist. In the book example, the bookstore owner need not continue to be present for us to understand that the book in our

15

possession was once in the bookstore owner's possession. If we are tailoring an item of clothing, the person need not be present for us to understand that the work we are doing is intended for another. In all of these understandings, we are aware not only of our own concerns but also of the concerns of Others. We will not trespass on another's field (Heidegger makes a point of saying that we walk outside it, not on it), and we are aware of our duty toward a customer if we are tailoring the customer's clothing. (118) Our interactions with Others are guided by our understanding of Others' Dasein; they are real people with real concerns. What's more, we understand Others as Dasein-with, and those Others understand us as Dasein-with; (121) even understanding oneself is grounded in Dasein-with because we are always Being-with Others. (123-124) We have an ongoing primordial relationship with Others.

In the same way in which our environment is made manifest through our dealings in the world, other people also are made manifest to us. However, because other people are Dasein like us, our comportment toward them and their significance to us are very different compared to entities. This difference profoundly influences the development of Self, individual identity—what is chosen to be shown to other people—and the interpretation of events and people in our environment. In terms of Blattner's definition of Dasein's self-understanding mentioned at the beginning of this book, other people have a profound effect on how Dasein understands itself. The source of meaning for Dasein are particular other Dasein and the society at large because, as Dreyfus says, all people are interconnected, and people function and move in a common environmental whole.[13]

It is this Dasein-with existential character of Being-with Others that is central to Dasein understanding itself because the most proximal existential connections that any person has are with other people. Dreyfus says Heidegger believed that humans begin to exist as they are socialized into the understanding of what it is to be human as contained in social practices.[14] Each Dasein must understand itself within its culture, and Dasein develops

---

[13] Dreyfus, *Being-in-the-world*, 142.
[14] Dreyfus, *Being-in-the-world*, 23.

its possibilities in terms of the society of Dasein in which it dwells. Thus, the "who" of a person is a shared social activity.[15]

Since, as Heidegger stated in regard to equipment, the movement of de-severance that lights up something is related to our involvements, we can say the same is true in regard to people. Extending Ortega's pencil example from earlier, if I go to a store to buy a pencil, I survey a box of pencils and choose a pencil to buy, making it my pencil. In Heideggerian language, I engaged in circumspective concern and de-severed that particular pencil and brought it close to me. The economic and legal transaction of purchasing a pencil has the ontological consequence of making an entity that was once distant and present-at-hand to being close and ready-to-hand equipment. We can see something similar in regard to dealing with people. If I go to a reception and survey the people there and choose someone with whom I wish to strike up a conversation, I am attempting to make someone distant from me closer to me by engaging him in conversation. This example is different from choosing a pencil in two ways. The first is obvious—a person is not a pencil, or, as Heidegger would say, another Dasein cannot be something ready-to-hand. The second way, though less obvious, is equally important—I must say "attempting" to bring him close to me because, unlike the pencil, she is Dasein possessing his own set of involvements and concerns, and he could avoid my attempts to bring him close.

The fact that another person could resist my attempts to talk to him or her does not negate the existential reality that he or she is "lit up" for me in that I am focusing my attention on him or her. This lighting up is a real feature of Dasein, even if it does not affect the object of my intention. However, people are affected by the intentions of other people, and they are frequently aware of this. If we notice someone looking at us, we almost cannot help but include that person in our involvements, even if for no longer than a brief irritation. We need not take that realization in the ways that Sartre, de Beauvoir, or Lacan do to understand that a person's

---

[15] This is from Dreyfus's "Interpreting Heidegger on Das Man." I find Dreyfus's comparisons of Heidegger and Wittgenstein on shared social activity to be mostly right and Olafson's critique of it in "Heidegger a'la Wittgenstein" mostly unconvincing except for his valid accusation that Dreyfus unjustifiably assimilates Heidegger's account of human being to the later-Wittgenstein's theory of language as rule governed.

involvements are shaped profoundly by the involvements of other people. We also need not consider the collective involvements of Others (what Heidegger calls "das Man") as a negative tyranny[16] or our response to it as a distortion of our being.[17] I am not suggesting these interpretations have no merit, only that they are not the only possible ones. For example, if we stop at a stop sign, it is because we are aware of the involvements of Others—they could be wanting to pass through that intersection at the same time we do. It would be too simplistic to attribute our stopping as exclusively subservient—there is also, at times, genuine concern for the interests of other people in our actions. The analysis of human actions is complicated by the multifaceted and interrelated system of human involvements.

Toward a Heideggerian Theory of Individual and Social Identity

We now start to bring together these concepts. Individual beliefs, actions, and identity are formed from the equiprimordial factors of each person's own mineness and Being-in-the-world. Each one of us forms an existential world—a personal region—of our own from the public world we share with other people. Within this personal region, we light up entities and people who reflect our involvements. In terms of human interaction, people are influenced by the people around them—individuals and the greater society—and they respond to these influences in terms of their own involvements within the larger context of public involvements. Therefore, each person is Being-in-the-world as Being toward the world in the ways that matter to that person in response to the world in which he or she finds him- or herself. A social group's identity is formed through the synergy of the Being-in of its members. Heidegger says toward the beginning of Chapter V ("Being-in as Such"):

---

[16] As Carman says, "Das Man is, so to speak, Heidegger's anti-personification of the anonymous normativity that he thinks governs and in fact tyrannizes so much of Dasein's everyday understanding of itself and its world." (Carman, 213)
[17] As Olafson says, "(Das Man) could simply be a distorted modality of Mitsein in which we all systematically detour around one another and ourselves in our authentic capacity as Dasein." (Olafson,59.)

The phenomenon of the equiprimordiality of constitutive items has often been disregarded in ontology, because of a methodologically unrestrained tendency to derive everything and anything from some simple 'primal ground.' (131)

A person's Being-in-the-world is grounded in equiprimordial items—mineness, involvements, and experiences. A person's individual lifeworld is formed through these equally fundamental items.

This equiprimordial foundation can enhance our philosophical explorations. In ethics, we can acknowledge possibilities of both human self-interest and altruism, both social influences and free moral agency. Social and political theory are enhanced by a realization of the public space being the collection of personal regions projected into it. This collective nature leads us to issues of how personal regions (belief systems) are formed and how social ideologies are formed and operate, which can be helpful in critical theory examination of social institutions, oppression, and freedom. We could even, within epistemology, explore the possibility of the equiprimordiality of human perception as informed and interpreted by mineness and Being-in-the-world.

In terms of issues within Heidegger's own philosophy, we can from this foundation fruitfully consider the issues of authenticity, care, temporality, das Man, Ereignis, Ge-stell, and others. It is in lighting up other people that Heidegger's concepts of everydayness, authenticity, and das Man can be understood. Such an interpretation of das Man perhaps can give us some insight into the nature of oppression, how ideologies are constructed and perpetuated, how propaganda works, and more.

We can take this as a starting point for an analysis of social interaction that could shed light on social behavior both positive and deviant and the basic structures of society. Heidegger did not pursue this path in *Being and Time*, opting instead to pursue an analytic of self-understanding—but the path is open to us. That path begins with acknowledging the "where" of Dasein's Being-in-the-world: Being-sphere.

Being-sphere

The conceptual building blocks discussed in the first section led us to the concept of Being-sphere. Dasein is the type of Being that we are, Being-in-the-world is the grounding of our Being, and Being-sphere is where the happening of Dasein's presence in the world happens and is the limited but dynamically open "where" of Dasein's Being-in-the-world. Being-sphere is "Being" in that it is an existentiale of Dasein, and it is "sphere"—meant in the sense of a "sphere of influence"—in that it is an existential region centered on Dasein that phenomenologically expresses how Dasein is Being-in-the-world. Being-sphere is how individual people are situated in the world and the region from which they interact with the world.

The world itself is Dasein's general background, but in what kind of existential place do Dasein's experiences and responses to the world occur? Jeff Malpas expresses what we are looking for:

> To understand or to interpret is thus to be engaged with things in the world within a certain open but bounded "space" of possibilities; it is to be located within a unitary but differentiated "region," each element of which is interconnected and mutually defining; it is to encounter oneself only inasmuch as one also encounters others, and inasmuch as one also encounters things.18

Being-sphere is this "open but bounded 'space' of possibilities [...] located within a unitary but differentiated 'region'" to which Malpas referred and what he also called "a certain open realm in which, not only things, but we ourselves are disclosed and come to presence—in which we are gathered together with the things around us."[19] I will argue that Being-sphere is the existential distinction of Dasein from other entities that we can identify phenomenologically as an individual's sense of "mine." In short, Being-sphere is existentially *where* Dasein is as it is in its everyday Being-in-the-world and the region of its involvements and possibilities.

Dasein is an entity immersed in a world that is always perceived by Dasein in terms of its involvements in the world (67). We do not encounter mere

---

[18] Malpas, Jeff, *Heidegger and the Thinking of Place*, Cambridge, MA, MIT Press, 2012, 204.

[19] Malpas, Jeff, *Heidegger's Topology,* Cambridge, MA, MIT Press, 2006, 15. My concept of Being-sphere is similar to Malpas's philosophy of place but unlike it in that my concept of Being-sphere is not restricted to physical spatiality.

"things" but "things invested with value" (68). Mostly, we interact with "equipment" (objects ready-to-hand), entities that we use and understand in terms of our assignments of them (68). Heidegger identifies where equipment belongs as a region, defined by the totality of involvements for which the equipment is intended to be used (104). But Heidegger's concept of regions is limited to physical objects in physical space, which is the logical consequence of his definition of a region as the place of equipment.[20] However, if a region is based on equipment, and equipment is defined by the involvements of Dasein, then a region must entail more than the physical location of entities. Heidegger's analysis is weighted toward consideration of the entities that receive meaning more than toward the meaning-holding Dasein. This observation does not invalidate Heidegger's thoughts about equipment and regions, but it points to an incompleteness in his theory. A region's "spatiality of the totality of equipment" has its unity "through that totality-of-involvements in-accordance-with-the-world" (104), but the totality-of-involvements in-accordance-with-the-world cannot be reduced to the spatiality of the totality of equipment without entering into circular reasoning. Equipment does not determine its involvements; equipment has its significance in the "for-the-sake-of-which" of Dasein's involvements (111, 123). Dasein's involvements are related to and affected by equipment and regions, but not completely determined by them. Therefore, the ontological reality in regions is formed by the society of Dasein, not equipment.

Just as equipment belongs somewhere (102), Dasein's involvements belong somewhere. This existential place is Being-sphere. Being-sphere, like a region, is laid out by Dasein with regard to possibilities of Dasein's Being. Heidegger's description of regions is incomplete because there is more to Dasein's Being-in-the-world than its use of equipment in regions (104). I do not suggest that Heidegger is wrong in what he says, but he misses an opportunity to say more about Dasein. Equipment is a vital part of Dasein's Being-in-the-world, but the world where Dasein dwells is more than a region delineated by equipment. Dasein's involvements also include other Dasein, personal and social values, and understandings and interpretations, all of which Dasein places in relation to its involvements. Therefore, the existential spaces that are regions are more than the world of material objects in physical space; regions are a mode of Dasein's existence where Dasein works out its involvements.

---

[20] Heidegger sees even the "there" of resoluteness in terms of physical objects in physical space: the "Situation," which, he says, is spatial (299).

21

We recognize Being-sphere when we recast Heidegger's regions as a state of Being of Dasein that includes Dasein's involvements. I stress "state of Being" because (1) Being-sphere is an existentiale of Dasein—Dasein is not Dasein without Being-sphere— and (2) Being-sphere is the existential space in which Dasein dwells and through which Dasein interacts with the world. Being-sphere is not a product of perception or reflection; it is the existential space where perceptions and reflections occur. The concept of Being-sphere includes Heidegger's concept of *Lichtung* (133, 170), the clearing that is Dasein's field of disclosedness or happening of truth.[21] Dreyfus holds that the clearing is Dasein's "situation as organized around its activity,"[22] which is true if we take "situation" to mean a state of Being of Dasein. The clearing is the Da of Dasein[23]; as Heidegger says, "Being-in-the-world it is cleared in itself, not through any other entity, but in such a way that it is itself the clearing" (133). The clearing is also Dasein's knowing—the place "that allows the emergence of things into presence"[24] enabling Dasein to appropriate them (170). Being-sphere is a distinct clearing, the place of the individual's "mine," within the totality of social space. Most importantly, the clearing of Being-sphere is the place where events of signification and understanding are possible for an individual Dasein. What individuals perceive as truth and meaning occur within the clearing that is Being-sphere. The clearing is what makes experience and understanding possible for Dasein because it is where Dasein's specific perceptions of the world are illuminated (133).[25] Dasein has an understanding through "standing in the clearing of presence" (204). Dasein's understandings within the clearing of Being-sphere are personal, but they are not arbitrary or illusory—each Dasein is unique in its experiences and unique in its responses to the world. *Lichtung* acknowledges the clearing of Dasein's knowing, and the concept of Being-sphere goes beyond *Lichtung* by also acknowledging the clearing of Dasein's

---

[21] Malpas, *Heidegger and the Thinking of Place*, 3.

[22] Dreyfus, Hubert L, *Being-in-the-World: A Commentary on Heidegger's* Being and Time, *Division I*, Cambridge, MA, MIT Press, 1991, 265.

[23] Stapleton, Timothy, "Dasein as Being in the World," Davis, Bret W. (ed.), *Martin Heidegger: Key Concepts*, Durham, UK, Acumen, 2010, 1-16, 44-56; 51.

[24] Malpas, *Heidegger and the Thinking of Place*, 19.

[25] Wrathall interprets the clearing as what makes some possibilities possible because it also "keeps back" other possibilities—the illumination reveals some possibilities by concealing others. Wrathall, Mark A., "Unconcealment," *Blackwell Companion to Heidegger*, Malden, MA, Blackwell Publishing, 2005, 337-357; 356.

individuated involvements and responses. The rest of the book will attempt to flesh out these acknowledgments.

The concept of Being-sphere is not imagining a new entity or realm; it is a phenomenological explanation of Dasein's presence and functioning in the world. What Being-sphere signifies is not a theoretically designated concept[26] but a philosophy of existential place. The importance of place is crucial to the philosophy of Being-sphere, but the notions of place in such philosophers as Malpas[27] and Henri Lefebvre[28] do not exhaust the possibilities of Being-sphere. Dasein dwells in Being-sphere, and its concernful dealings with the world occur in Being-sphere. Being-sphere then *is* Dasein's Being-in-the-world specific to the individual Dasein—how Dasein dwells in, perceives, experiences, and acts within its environment, including Dasein's network of meaningful relations and its understanding of its place and actions within the wider world (117).

I will attempt to disclose the ontological structure of Being-sphere through a phenomenological analysis of how it contains Dasein's knowing, Dasein's situatedness, Dasein's significance and comportment, and Dasein's identity relations. I will discuss each in turn and then show how Being-sphere is a concept that reveals how Dasein is individuated.

Dasein's Knowing in Being-sphere

Descartes' concept of the knowing subject has long been a target of philosophical criticism. The Cartesian subject is insufficient to explain human experience, but rather than continue flogging the dead horse of the Cartesian subject, it is better to find a suitable substitute for the concept because Descartes' mistake was an understandable one. It must, as Kant said, be possible

---

[26] I refer here to Heidegger's rejection of "theoretically concocted explanations" (119).
[27] I fundamentally agree with Malpas that Heidegger's work is a philosophy of place (p. 43, *Heidegger and the Thinking of Place*), but I find his first book on the subject, *Heidegger's Topology*, too restricted to physical place, and his second book *Heidegger and the Thinking of Place* is focused on his later writings. My sense is that Being-sphere is compatible with Malpas's topology as I have indicated in several places in this book
[28] Henri Lefebvre's philosophy of place in his books *The Production of Space* and *Everyday Life in the Modern World* focuses on the social production of social space but does not directly address individual existential space. Lefebvre, Henri, *Everyday Life in the Modern World*, Rabinovitch, Sacha (tr.), New York, Harper Torchbooks, 1971. Lefebvre, Henri, *The Production of Space*, Nicholson-Smith, Donald (tr.), Oxford, UK, Blackwell Publishers, 1991.

for the "I think" to accompany our thoughts.[29] This "I" signifies something that cannot be dismissed as illusion. The responses that Dasein has are made by something, and not by a homunculus, or similar such conception of individualizing the human being as something separate from the world, but by a being who dwells in the world. Heidegger correctly stresses Dasein's mineness—the "I am" that "has always made some sort of decision as to the way in which it is in each case mine" (42) or what Mark Okrent interprets as the argument that if an agent is in the world and intending toward and using entities, then that agent also intends herself as the for-the-sake-of-which herself her intentions are organized—the I as the "for-the-sake-of-which" being a necessary condition for other kinds of intentions.[30] Whatever view we may hold of how it is that an individual thinks and acts, what underlies any and all such theorizing must be the recognition that a particular being is having those particular thoughts and committing those particular actions. What sort of being?

To address this question, we turn to Heidegger's discussion of the phenomenology of Dasein's knowing the world in which he gives a different answer to Descartes' question of what this thinking thing is. Heidegger rejects the idea that knowing is a subject-object relation (60-62). Such a view of knowledge presumes that the self is an isolated subject, a cogito in an inner sphere,[31] and, as Heidegger points out, has a problem explaining how an isolated subject can make its way out of its inner sphere into the outer sphere of the world to know objects in the outside world (60, 62, 96-97). Heidegger says that rather than viewing knowing as achieving "transcendence" over a relation between subject and object, knowing should be understood as "a kind of Being which belongs to Dasein's Being-in-the-world" (61). When I am knowing

---

[29] Kant, Immanuel, *Critique of Pure Reason*, Smith, Norman Kemp (tr.), London, Macmillan, 1968, B131. Acknowledging that my thought belongs to me does not commit us to a representationalist view of knowledge. The "I think" remains a distinctive feature of Dasein's mental life. Heidegger's conclusion from his discussion of Kant's "I think" (319-321) is that *"In saying 'I', Dasein expresses itself as Being-in-the-world"* (321, emphasis his).

[30] Okrent, Mark, "The 'I Think' and the For-the-Sake-of-Which," Crowell, Steven and Malpas, Jeff (eds.), *Transcendental Heidegger*, Stanford, CA, Stanford University Press, 2007, 165.

[31] "Perhaps the most basic Cartesian assumption is that human life goes on 'inside', not 'outside'. There is a special sphere in which human existence takes place, which we may call the mind, the subject, consciousness, the ego or the self." Polt, Richard, *Heidegger: An Introduction*, Ithaca, NY, Cornell University Press, 1999, 55.

something about the world, I do not leave my inner sphere and return to my "cabinet of consciousness" with the booty of knowledge I have obtained (62). I am always out there amidst the objects. In looking at the world, Heidegger says that Dasein is amidst entities within-the-world (61). In knowing, Heidegger says, "the Dasein which knows remains outside, and it does so as Dasein" (62).[32] However, knowing "is not some external characteristic, it must be inside" (60). Knowing cannot be in what is known but must be in the knower. This apparent contradiction of knowing being both inner and outer is resolved by the realization that my knowing anything, even myself, is grounded in my dwelling in and being a part of the world, amidst it, and this grounding is constitutive of Dasein's Being (61, 124) and points us to Being-sphere.

The concept of Being-sphere enables us to see how Dasein meaningfully engages and experiences the world. Heidegger remarks that in experiences

> Something does happen... I am fully present in my 'I'... It is an experience proper to me and so do I see it... Lived experience does not pass in front of me like a thing, but I appropriate it to myself, and it appropriates itself according to its essence.[33]

Experience is a happening proper to Dasein in which appropriation, or knowing, relates Dasein to something in the world and makes it its own. The happening of knowing happens somewhere, and that somewhere is not a Cartesian subject but the state of Being in which Dasein gathers its events of knowing and its relations with the world—a clearing in the midst of the world.

It is important to distinguish the term "knowing" from "knowledge." Heidegger is correct that the problem of knowledge presupposes that the subject can transcend itself, whereas his conception of knowing as being amidst the world does not have that presupposition (61). We should also keep in mind that Heidegger's Being-in-the-world is far broader than factual knowledge and encompasses all the ways in which Dasein comports itself toward the world.[34] An example of this:

> Dasein's facticity is such that its Being-in-the-world has always dispersed itself or even split itself up into definite ways of Being-

---

[32] The act of Dasein understanding its world is inherently outside itself as Heidegger mentions that "as Being-in-the world (Dasein) is already 'outside' when it understands" (162).

[33] Heidegger, *Toward the Definition of Philosophy*, 63 (*GA* 56/57:75); quoted from Malpas, *Topology*, 58.

[34] Descartes, René, *Meditations on First Philosophy*, Second Meditation.

in. The multiplicity of these is indicated by the following examples: having to do with something, producing something, attending to something and looking after it, making use of something, giving something up and letting it go, undertaking, accomplishing, evincing, interrogating, considering, discussing, determining. All these ways of Being-in have concern as their kind of Being (56-57).

This is similar to Descartes' list of what he considers thinking: "Well, then, what am I? A thing that thinks. What is that? A thing that doubts, understands, affirms, denies, wants, refuses, and also imagines and senses."

Dasein is not only in the world, it *knows* the world, and Heidegger observes that this "knowing is a mode of Being of Dasein as Being-in-the-world" (61-62). Knowing the world is phenomenologically understood as a comportment, a taking over of a viewpoint in encountering the world that is "the mode of dwelling autonomously [amidst] entities within-the-world" (61). Heidegger's use of "autonomously" does not equate Dasein with a Cartesian subject or a free-floating "I" but suggests instead the important realization that Dasein is, as Taylor termed it, an "engaged agent."[35] Engaged agents are distinct autonomous beings that operate within a background, whose distinct world is shaped by their mode of being.[36] Taylor explains that the engaged agent is "world shaped"[37] and differentiates the concept from what he calls the philosophical position of "disengagement," examples of which he gives as Descartes' dualism and Hobbes's mechanism.[38] His definition of engaged agency as "that agency whose experience is made intelligible only by being placed in the context of the kind of agency it is"[39] points to Being-sphere as the existential place where context confers intelligibility in the Being of the engaged agent. I contend that the background that Taylor speaks of in his excellent paper is Being-sphere, which is the nonrepresentational background of experience that individuals are familiar with, more even than they are with the world itself. I think if we stay with the world as the primordial background, we are left struggling to get beyond concepts of disengagement, but Being-sphere gives us

---

[35] Taylor, Charles, "Engaged Agency and Background in Heidegger," Guignon, Charles B. (ed.), *The Cambridge Companion to Heidegger*, Cambridge, UK, Cambridge University Press, 1993, 317-326; 328.
[36] Taylor, 318-319.
[37] Taylor, 318.
[38] Taylor, 322-324.
[39] Taylor, 325.

the individual's primordial background of engagement. The agent is not a detached subject who has knowledge about entities outside; he or she has a comportment toward the entities that he or she is in the midst of. This knowing comportment forms Dasein's understanding of its place in the world, constituting significance. We will deal more with the importance of significance and comportment later.

The concept of Being-sphere captures the importance of knowing as Being-amidst-the-world and how knowing has the character of being both inner and outer to itself. Dasein's events of knowing must occur not in a separate inner sphere but in something that is amidst the world, or it would not be Being-in-the-world. But it cannot be in the world in the same way as an entity present-at-hand because that would make it not Dasein. Thus, as Mulhall states, "insofar as we think of our commerce with the world as a relation between subject and objects, then Dasein is the Being of this 'between'."[40] Dasein comports itself not outwardly from an inner sphere toward entities but in the midst of those entities. Dasein is capable of internal reflection, but mostly it dwells "outside" amidst entities. It takes its possibilities from the world that it continually discovers through its own distinct experiences (194). In Dasein's everyday dealings with the world, its Being-in-the-world is both inside and outside Dasein amidst the world.

Being-sphere is the distinct existential standpoint from which Dasein perceives and understands. This standpoint is a dynamic, not static, mode of being. Spatially, Dasein is only temporarily located in its current place. Temporally, Dasein is always in the current moment, but its experiences and responses are not restricted by the current moment—it has memories of its past, thoughts of possibilities in the future, and the ability to imagine alternative scenarios. As Dreyfus expresses it, "I move from being in one situation to being in the next by shifts in my readiness, which is itself shaped by years of experience with how situations typically evolve."[41] Being in a situation (not to be confused with Heidegger's special term "Situation" (299-300)) must existentially reside somewhere, and this state of readiness is key in recognizing Dasein's knowing as existentially residing in Being-sphere. Dasein's current knowing, its past experiences and responses, plus its ability to project itself

---

[40] Mulhall, Stephen, *Routledge Philosophy Guidebook to Heidegger and Being and Time*, London, Routledge, 1996, 75.
[41] Dreyfus, 119.

toward the future and direct its actions toward the world form an ever-present specific but dynamic Being (144). Dasein dynamically responds intelligently and purposefully from an existentially distinct place to stand not separate from the world but amidst the world. It is in this standpoint, "a kind of dwelling" (61), that Dasein deals with the world, perceives, directs itself toward things, makes assignments, and confers significance to the things it experiences.

Being-sphere is thus a state of Being formed in the dynamic interaction of Dasein with its environment. Being-sphere is the existential place formed by Dasein's dwelling in the world because Dasein is not the "I myself" but the "I interacting with the world." This ontological structure of Being-sphere—that Dasein is outside itself dynamically considering the world—has given rise to two persistent illusions. One is the solipsistic illusion that we exist as a Cartesian subject—a homunculus that peers out from our cloister at the world that is separate from us. The other is the reductionist illusion that we are nothing but the effects of external forces, either materialistic or cultural. Both illusions are based on taking a partial truth as the whole truth of Dasein—the former, placing too much emphasis on Dasein as participant; the latter, placing too much emphasis on Dasein as recipient. The full truth is that Dasein interacts with the world as both a recipient and a participant and that Being-sphere is the existential place of this interaction. Dasein is inextricably immersed in a world that it continually experiences, and experiences are subjective in that experiences of the world are experienced by that particular individual and no one else, and that individual does not experience any other individual's experiences. It is from Dasein's distinct experiences which constitute and affect its dealings with the world that it responds to the world and thus is locus of participation in the world. Dasein's experiences and responses become and remain a part of Dasein's Being-sphere.

Dasein's Situatedness in Being-sphere

If we do not leave an inner sphere to go into another sphere to experience the world, where *are* we when we encounter the world? To say "in the world" is too general because Dasein is a distinct entity with a distinct situatedness in the world. Dasein's physical spatial-temporal situation is also insufficient because Dasein is not in the world like water is in a glass (54), which has implications for both what the world is to Dasein and what Dasein is. Heidegger observes

28

that Dasein organizes regions in terms of left/right, front/back, and up/down, which are aspects of an individual's relative orientation, not features of space independent of Dasein (109-110). Relative orientation shows that Dasein's spatiality pragmatically reflects its individual involvements, but it does not fully capture Dasein's Being-in-the-world. Just as we cannot reduce Dasein's Being-in-the-world to spatial coordinates, we cannot reduce Dasein's Being-in-the-world to its orientation in space no matter how subjectively conceived.[42] Physical space is only one aspect of Dasein's world and what Dasein is (113).

Dasein is in the world as a Being of concernful involvement that projects itself into the world in terms of its own involvements and projects. We can say, as Heidegger does, that the Being-in-the-world of Dasein is "Being-outside" itself amidst the entities that it encounters (62).[43] But Dasein is amidst the world engaged with it in terms of its individual involvements and individual knowing. We can more fully address the importance of individual involved engagement by expanding Heidegger's purely physical spatiality concept of regions into the spatiality plus involvements concept of Being-sphere. Heidegger's concept of regions needs expansion because, though Dasein-in-the-world is a locus of spatiality, Dasein-in-the-world is also a locus of significance, and we need to reflect that with the concept of Being-sphere.

The concept of Being-sphere includes how individual Dasein proximally thinks of space and entities in terms of significance. Dasein, being that entity whose Being is an issue for it, possesses the kind of being that has concerns, and these concerns compel it to respond to the world in which it cannot help but be involved (56-57). Dasein's concernful, involved awareness of the world and its situation compel it to respond to address its concerns, and this involvement is ontologically definitive for its Being (84). Dasein always has "for-the-sake-of-whiches"—what most people would call "goals." To accomplish these goals, Dasein must involve itself in the world by responding to its environment with actions working toward its goals. Dasein, being a concernful being immersed in the world, must choose and act for the sake of accomplishing its own projects, and it appropriates equipment (objects of significance) to suit its own involvements (69).

---

[42] Dreyfus describes it as "a moving center of pragmatic activity in the midst of a shared world." Dreyfus, 164. This is a good description but remains limited to physical spatiality.

[43] Or, as Dreyfus says, "Dasein outside itself, formed by shared practices." Dreyfus, 163.

We can see the role of significance in Dasein's forming of regions when we take up Heidegger's example of the workshop. He pictures the workshop as a region that makes possible appropriate places for the hammer, the saw, the workbench, and so on. The workshop has been laid out by someone with regard to possibilities of Being—the region that makes the tools available for involvement. The workshop is a region, and on the basis of the tools within it and our understanding of other Dasein, we would recognize it as a carpenter's workshop. But for Dasein there is an important difference between "a carpenter's workshop" and "my workshop" or "my friend's workshop." These terms are referring not only to a particularity of place but also to a particular significance attached to the workshop. The significance of "my workshop" is of a different character than "a carpenter's workshop" or even "the carpenter's workshop at 42 High Street." Although we often encounter entities and regions that are not particularly significant to us, that which is closest and most significant to us has a deeper significance beyond placing an entity in its proper place according to social norms.

Capturing this difference in significance requires the additional concept of Being-sphere that expands Heidegger's concept of regions. Dasein's concernful involvement assigns a greater weight of significance to particular objects and places than it assigns to other objects and places. Heidegger's concept of regions includes the context of involvements (104), but it centers on the idea of a region as a place where equipment belongs (102-103), and equipment is defined by social assignments (68-69). I think these definitions are correct but insufficient to explain the phenomenon of "my friend's workshop." In its dealings, individual Dasein comes across what society defines as a workshop, but what makes it "my friend's" is not the ontic workshop or society's assignments, but the significance assigned to it by the individual Dasein.

Just as a region makes it possible for equipment to belong somewhere (103), Being-sphere makes it possible for Dasein's understandings and involvements to belong somewhere. This somewhere is not spatial, but in Dasein's involvements. The difference between *a* workshop and *my friend's* workshop is that my friend's workshop is part of my Being-sphere—it matters to me in a way that other workshops do not. Both workshops are regions, but my involvements relate to my friend's workshop not to the other workshop; it is therefore "real" to me in a way that the other workshop is not. I do not deny that the other workshop actually exists, but it does not have a place within my

30

involvements and thus is not a part of my thoughts, feelings, and life. The other workshop potentially could become part of my Being-sphere if my involvements change, just as my friend's workshop potentially could fall out of my involvements. The concept of Being-sphere must address this part of Dasein's Being-in-the-world, and it is to that which we now turn.

Dasein's Significance and Comportment in Being-sphere

We can see how Dasein's Being-sphere forms by using Heidegger's concept of de-severance and applying it to Dasein's knowing and its situatedness in Being-sphere. "De-severing amounts to making the farness vanish—that is, making the remoteness of something disappear, bringing it close" (105). Heidegger considers entities to be ontologically remote until they are brought close by a person—made available for involvement (105). Heidegger says that Dasein is "essentially de-severant: it lets any entity be encountered close by as the entity which it is" and that "in Dasein there lies an essential tendency towards closeness" (105). De-severance is thus a constitutive state of Dasein's Being in which Dasein constitutes its world in terms of its involvements (105). That de-severance involves more than procuring entities and placing them in a region for use is hinted at by Heidegger in his discussion of the relativity of remoteness and how remoteness is not distance. He gives examples of the expressions "a good walk" and "a stone's throw," which, though not mathematical measurements, still reference physical space (105). He observes that the measure "half an hour" is not meant as officially thirty minutes but as a "duration which has no [precise] 'length' at all" (106). But what makes either a pathway or time either long or short when it comes before us? Considering something as long or short is, from our consideration of it, de-severing it. Heidegger speaks of Dasein de-severing something not in terms of space but in terms of its "concernful Being-in-the-world—that is, towards whatever is proximally encountered in such Being" (107). I think this is right, but Heidegger's next step is to turn this line of reasoning back to equipment in physical space (107-110). This move, to what Dreyfus calls "existential spatiality,"[44] captures something meaningful to Dasein's Being-in-the-world, but Dasein's Being-in-the-world is not exhausted by the existential aspects of

---

[44] Drefyus, 137-140.

physical space, so something remains missing from Heidegger's analysis. Being-sphere acknowledges that de-severance involves all of Dasein's activity, not just use of physical equipment. Heidegger offers an example of de-severance outside of physical equipment:

> But certain ways in which entities are discovered in a purely cognitive manner also have the character of bringing them close. [...] All the ways in which we speed things up, as we are more or less compelled to do today, push us on towards the conquest of remoteness. With the 'radio', for example, Dasein has so expanded its everyday environment that it has accomplished a de-severance of the 'world's de-severance which, in its meaning for Dasein, cannot yet be visualized. (105)

It is obvious that anything that is capable of being the subject of consciousness is capable of being de-servered and brought close.

The de-severance of remoteness is, at times, a matter of physical space, but it is also a matter of what Malpas calls "bringing into salience" [45]—though I will stay with Heidegger's term "significance." In terms of physical space, an individual forms his or her region by bringing entities close and placing them in ways that are meaningful to him or her. But physical equipment in physical space is not the only significance at work here. De-severance also forms Dasein's Being-sphere by bringing involvements, ideas, and possibilities into significance—the things of Dasein's knowing—and Dasein's knowing occurs in Being-sphere. This "bringing into significance" is not a matter of separating out a personal space from within public space but a matter of opening one's involvements to physical entities and nonphysical ideas and bringing them close. For example, the game of baseball is a cultural artifact available to all but significant only to those who are involved with it. I am a fan of baseball, but my wife is not, and this contributes differently to our respective Being-spheres. How

---

[45] Malpas, *Topology,* 76. However, Malpas interprets the salience of de-severance as meaning an awareness of spatial distance—his example is becoming aware that a book he wants is beyond his reach (p. 91). Malpas restricts de-severance within his conception of a holistic equipmental structure of physical objects in physical space. But spatial ordering is just one way in which Dasein de-severs. Yes, if I reach for a book, I have de-severed it from its spatial background. But what if I think of that same book without reaching for it? Malpas partially recognizes the point in acknowledging that spatiality is related temporally in terms of our "activities, tasks, and ends," which is "being-there's own existential spatiality" (p. 92). He similarly interprets involvement as tied to a mode of physical spatiality that is oriented by Dasein's active engagement with the world (p. 126) and "equipmental spatiality" as "related back to a particular bodily space" (p. 137).

my team does is important to me, but it is not important to my wife, so the score of their last game is part of my Being-sphere but not my wife's. Even when I tell her "my team won," she remains unaffected. That my team won is objectively true, but its significance differs in our Being-spheres. I de-sever—bring close—the game because of my involvements and significance; my wife does not. This is an example of how Being-sphere and what is within it are specific to the individual.

Another illustration of the importance of significance can be found in Dreyfus's contention that Heidegger does not consistently distinguish the fact that Dasein can only de-sever entities that are present in a public space prior to the movement of de-severance. If we grant to Dreyfus that Heidegger is guilty of this inconsistency, the problem is not resolved by Dreyfus's attempt to make de-severance even more tied to physical space.[46] True, as Dreyfus says, public space comes prior to de-severance, and Dasein's de-severance can only involve an entity that is available to it in public space.[47] Existential spatiality is grounded not only in public space, however, but also in Dasein's concern for its projects and its interactions. De-severance is an interaction with physical space with its basis in Dasein's involvements, and we must include both the de-severed entity and individual Dasein's involvements in our description of de-severance. Individual involvements and physical entities are best seen in a kind of balance in our understanding of Dasein's de-severance—a symbiosis of involvements and equipment that dynamically support each other. If a hammer belongs on a workbench, it is not because of the hammer or workbench but because of Dasein's involvements, even though the involvement is a public one given to Dasein by social norms. When individual Dasein places a hammer on a workbench, it is not an end in itself but the means through which individual Dasein attempts to achieve its projects. Why is the acquaintance at a distance closer to us than the street that is directly beneath us (107)? Because the acquaintance matters to us more than the street does at that moment. Distance is not an issue of time or space alone but of meaning and value. As Heidegger says:

> Circumspective concern decides as to the closeness and farness of
> what is proximally ready-to-hand environmentally. Whatever this

---

[47] Drefyus, 131-140.

> concern dwells [amidst] beforehand is what is closest, and this is
> what regulates our de-severances (107).

Dreyfus misunderstands this passage in his commentary[48] because he seems to restrict de-severance to an exclusively spatial assessment. But de-severance is a matter of concernful dealing as Heidegger states—assigning significance to equipment and ideas within Being-sphere. Dasein navigates through space by using de-severance, and Heidegger is not confusing ontic distance with ontological de-severance but pointing out their distinction—and what creates that distinction is significance. The importance of existential distance as assigning significance is key to a phenomenology of Dasein's knowing in Being-sphere because de-severance is the way that Dasein encounters and appropriates anything in the world.

Heidegger ascribes assignments and significance to a holistic totality of involvements, an emphasis that implies, if not necessitates, that significance occur on a social level. Although this is largely correct, the problem with this view is that social significance is largely undifferentiated, a reality that Heidegger expresses in his concept of *das Man*. Heidegger's conception of Dasein's everydayness places significance in social roles rather than in a defuse notion of society as a whole, but that only slightly narrows the undifferentiation. Placing significance in social roles makes sense, but there remains the problem of explaining how particular significances can be made manifest by an individual or why a particular Dasein would engage in a particular action.

Steven Crowell argues that Heidegger's answer to the problem of individual action is that significance is anchored in Dasein's very being as the sole authentic for-the-sake-of-which[49] (84). Crowell argues that Dasein is a being capable of not just merely conforming to norms but acting in light of them. To do so, Crowell says, Dasein measures a norm against a "meta-norm"— an act of first-person authority that grounds self-actions in a self-obligation to social norms, thus giving justifying reasons for its action.[50] Crowell's formulation is in keeping with Heidegger's notions of conscience and *das Man*, but it does not solve the problem of why a particular Dasein would engage in a particular action. Crowell moves the question from why Dasein acts in the face of social norms to why Dasein gives reason for its actions in the face of social

---

[48] Drefyus, 133-135.

[49] Crowell, Steven, "Subjectivity: Locating the First-Person in Being and Time," in *Inquiry*, 44:4 (2001) 433-454; 437-438.

[50] Crowell, 446.

norms, especially given that Crowell agrees with Heidegger that the reasons can be grounded only in social norms.[51] We still need an explanation for how and why Dasein would make a specific choice from among possibilities and commit to it, and we need the concept of Being-sphere to engage in the long process of crafting such an explanation. Applying the existential place of Being-sphere, we can start to ask how it is that Dasein, as an engaged agent dwelling autonomously in the world, can choose or not choose to adapt to social norms and other situations in which it finds itself. I will begin to address this large topic by discussing *das Man* and *Befindlichkeit* later in this book.

Saying that things are encountered through Being-sphere in terms of involvement denotes more than subjectivity; it clarifies the state of being of Dasein's Being-in-the-world. Subjectivity is the true world of Dasein, as Heidegger states:

> This 'subjectivity' perhaps uncovers the 'Reality' of the world at its most Real; it has nothing to do with 'subjective arbitrariness' or subjectivistic 'ways of taking' an entity which 'in itself' is otherwise. The circumspective de-severing of Dasein's everydayness reveals the Being-in-itself of the 'true world'—of that entity which Dasein, as something existing, is already [amidst].
> (106, emphasis his)

De-severance reveals the Being of the "true world"—the distinct world known to an individual Dasein. Dasein's world is not, as Wittgenstein defined, "all that is the case"[52]; it is, instead, the limited world of Dasein's experiences. The inherent finitude of Dasein's Being means it cannot know the totality of facts but only that to which it is exposed. The grasping of knowing can only grasp what is within its reach. But within the limits of its experience, Dasein de-severs in terms of its involvements, shrinking its world even further.

In terms of physical entities, Dasein places equipment within space to suit its involvements and considers the region created its own (103-104). But Heidegger applies the concept of de-severance almost exclusively to physical

---

[51] Crowell, 446-448. Crowell paraphrases Heidegger at *Being and Time*, 285 that "I 'take responsibility' for my facticity, 'own' it, make it my own through the 'choice of one possibility,'" accurately reflecting Heidegger's idea that authenticity is owning one's following of social norms.

[52] Wittgenstein, Ludwig, *Tractatus Logico-Philosophicus,* Pears, D.F. and McGuinness, B.F. (tr.), London, Routledge and Kegan Paul, 1961, proposition 1.0.

objects in physical space, yet Dasein's "true world" is also the values and ideas that correspond to physical objects in physical space. Through de-severance, Dasein brings close not only objects but also ideas, beliefs, communication, and other people to form Being-sphere. The concept of regions works well for a phenomenological analysis of tool use and three-dimensional social space, but it is inadequate for a phenomenological analysis of family ties, affiliations with groups and causes, what an individual understands is appropriate or not, and judgments on ethics, aesthetics, and values. Being-sphere includes these cultural artifacts because it is not reducible to either the physical or the mental but encompasses both, manifested and expressed in terms of Dasein's involvements. Dasein's de-severance is more than bringing close equipment; it is also how Dasein brings close significances and uses them to relate to the world.

Just as regions are laid out in terms of equipment for use, Being-sphere is laid out in terms of individual significance. Returning to the baseball example: I bring the game close into significance—and not necessarily the physical game but the idea of the game—and it becomes part of my Being-sphere whether I am physically present at the game or not. Within my distinct Being-sphere, I respond to the game in mental, emotional, and physical ways. Because my responses are related to my individual involvements, my responses are uniquely mine. When my team loses, I am affected by it, and that affectedness is mine alone to deal with, and that is reflected in my Being-sphere.

Being-sphere is the existential space where Dasein's comportments take place. Comportment is not what is perceived but "the way and manner of its being-perceived."[53] Macquarrie and Robinson explain that "The verb '*verhalten*' (comportment) can refer to any kind of behaviour or way of conducting oneself, even to the way in which one relates oneself to something else, or to the way one refrains or holds oneself back."[54] A comportment is Dasein's stance toward something; for example, Dasein takes a stand in comporting itself toward its being (41). We mentioned earlier that knowing is a comportment, and, just as knowing is both inner and outer to Dasein, so are comportments. Another

[53] Heidegger, *History of the Concept of Time: Prolegomena*, Bloomington, IN, Indiana University Press, 2009, 40.
[54] Macquarrie and Robinson in *Being and Time,* 23, fn. 1.

example of a comportment is being in a hurry. There is not a physical place called "hurry," but it is a behavior and a taking of a stance toward the world. Comportment is a being/doing/having in the state of Being that is Dasein's Being-sphere. A comportment is not a propositional intentional state but a prepropositional practical state.[55] Everyday comportment includes Dasein's practical entity-directed comportments, which is the behavior of grasping and de-severing entities within Being-sphere; the comportment, the de-severing, and the resulting knowing all involve significance.

Dasein encounters and dwells within a context of significance. Dasein lives in terms of significance and co-constitutes significance. Not every event and entity has a substantial significance, but significance is endemic to Dasein's Being. When an individual has concerns and involvements, this comportment necessarily creates significance. Significance is also related to de-severance in that de-severance alters Dasein's comportment toward what is de-severed. Once de-severed, the equipment, person, or idea becomes part of Dasein's knowing in Being-sphere and it has a significance to Dasein that it did not have before. This bringing into significance does not alter the object of de-severance, but it alters Dasein's Being-sphere, affecting its future perceptions and responses. De-severance thus plays a crucial role in individuating Dasein from other Dasein—the collective de-severances and significances of a life form a distinct Being-sphere.

We must add to the bringing-close of an entity the aspect of for-the-sake-of-which—the involvements that are present in Dasein's comportments—which Heidegger calls "understanding." As mentioned before, knowing is not knowledge, and similarly, understanding is not a rational capturing of booty but is, he says, Dasein projecting its possibilities: "Understanding is the existential Being of Dasein's own potentiality-for-Being; and it is so in such a way that this Being discloses in itself what its Being is capable of" (144). A particular passage of Heidegger's helps illustrate where we can place understanding:

> The character of understanding as projection is constitutive for Being-in-the-world with regard to the disclosedness of its existentially constitutive state-of-Being by which the factical potentiality-for-Being gets its leeway (145).

---

[55] Dreyfus, Hubert and Wrathall, Mark, "Martin Heidegger: An Introduction to His Thought, Work, and Life," *Blackwell Companion to Heidegger*, Malden, MA, Blackwell Publishing, 2005, 1-15, 6, 9.

The German word translated as "leeway" is *Spielraum*, which Dreyfus translates as "room for maneuver."[56] This "room for maneuver" is Dasein's Being-sphere. It is not "out there" in the world because the individual is maneuvering not in physical space but within his or her sphere of involvements. But it is not "within" an individual in the sense of a homunculus looking out at the world because Dasein is always Being-in-the-world. Being-sphere is the existential space within which Dasein works out its projects through an understanding of its possibilities and comportments toward the world in its involvements, bringing close into its Being-sphere what is significant to it in the same way it would place equipment into a region. From its Being-sphere and individual projects his or her responses out into the world. Being-sphere has leeway in that Dasein has room to respond within the limits of its Being-sphere. Those limits are crucial, because though Dasein is capable of responding to its possibilities, it finds its possibilities limited because it finds itself thrown into a world largely beyond its control (144). I will touch more on Dasein's responses when we apply Being-sphere to Heidegger's concept of *Befindlichkeit*.

So we can see that Being-sphere does not express any form of idealism but is an acknowledgment of what Being-in-the-world means for perception and individual responses. An individual Dasein, a person, perceives an entity and can respond to the entity upon perceiving it, so we are dealing with two ontological realities within Dasein's Being-sphere: perception and response. An example from John Haugeland helps explain this distinction: The difference between perceiving a pot and making a pot is that the potter must already have the look of the pot in mind prior to producing what does not already exist.[57] Haugeland is pointing out the distinction between *perceptual* comportments and *productive* comportments. The former is associated with grasping (knowing) what already exists and the latter with understanding what *can* exist. Individuals have comportment toward what they take in through perception and comportment toward what they put out through their productive activities.

With Haugeland, I am referring to the overall production that allows a piece of equipment to be ready-to-hand rather than specific physical actions that go into making the pot.[58] The physical actions are undertaken for-the-sake-of an

---

[56] Dreyfus, 186.
[57] Haugeland, John, "Letting Be," Crowell, Steven and Malpas, Jeff (eds.), *Transcendental Heidegger*, Stanford, CA, Stanford University Press, 2007, 93-103; 97.
[58] Haugeland, 97. "Genuine, successful *production* of a pot—that is, *finishing* it, and

involvement and are performed according to what the individual producer has in mind. The individual's involvement is the driving force behind the creation of the pot, and the productive comportment of that individual is the guiding force in the specifics of the production. That these significances and involvements do not appear *ex nihilo* but from out of Dasein's Being-in-the-world should be obvious. The past experiences of the individual producer form the horizon of possibilities for his or her involvements and significance. But we cannot forget that these experiences are influenced by the individual's comportments, which are not entirely given to the individual but are also produced by the individual. The individual is a locus of productive action. In creating a pot, Haugeland says, "the producer has to give it (arrange for it to have) the capacities and capabilities that it will need in order to be on its own"—the potter enables the pot to come into existence by using existing materials to make the pot able to be usable on its own when the potter is finished making it.[59] This process also applies to ideas. The individual's productive comportment is a response to the world that give ideas and entities new form or existence emerging from the leeway in Dasein's responses within its Being-sphere into the public sphere able to be experienced by others.

Dasein's leeway in Being-sphere includes Heidegger's discussion of interpretation,[60] which we can use to fill out the concept of Being-sphere even further. Heidegger speaks of interpretation grounded in a fore-having (150) and that any meaning that Dasein projects onto something "gets its structure from a fore-having, a fore-sight, and a fore-conception" (151). The nature of this fore-structure of understanding is not made entirely clear by Heidegger, but it seems that it is, as Gelvin concludes, an "existence-structure of the inquirer himself."[61] But what manner of existence-structure? I do not think Heidegger adequately characterizes it, nor do I think Gelvin's concept of "a mode of existence that reveals to Dasein its existence"[62] is adequate. The concept of Being-sphere is

---

letting it be—is something more like *letting go of* or *releasing it*: that is, handing it over to the customer. Or putting it in the cupboard, available to be used." (emphasis his)
[59] Haugeland, 97-98.
[60] I am aware that an argument can be made that Heidegger is thinking in ¶32 mostly in terms of the meaning of Being, but he also mentions interpretation of a table, a door, a carriage, and a bridge (149), so extending understanding and interpretation to everyday objects is certainly not out of bounds.
[61] Gelvin, Michael, *A Commentary on Heidegger's* Being and Time, *Revised Edition,* DeKalb, IL, Northern Illinois University Press, 1989, 90.

closer, even if not fully adequate, to characterizing Heidegger's fore-structure of Dasein, "the existential state of Being of the 'there'" and "the formal-existential framework of the disclosedness which belongs to understanding" of which Heidegger speaks.[63] Wrathall is right that understanding and interpretation are not brain states but ways of acting in the world.[64] Understanding and interpretation are proximally not rational reflection but Dasein's everyday responses from Being-sphere.[65] Dasein does not gaze at the world from outside it assessing it through propositional attitudes of belief, desire, and meaning. Dasein's understanding and interpretation are based on its involvements and identity relations amidst the world and thus is existential before it is cognitive. We do not throw a signification on some naked thing (150), but we do interpret things based on the fore-structure of experiences and responses—the totality of social and personal identities—that comprise our Being-sphere.

Dasein's Identity in Being-sphere

Ultimately, Dasein's situatedness is not the world itself but its set of relations to the world, which are relations of identity within Being-sphere. Dasein is a being that is concerned about its own being, but it is also the case that Dasein's identity is an issue for it. Identity is how Dasein *understands* its place and possibilities in the world, which differs from how Dasein *is* in the world. Even Dasein's experience of itself and its actions differs from how it understands itself and its actions—this understanding is its identity. By identity, I do not mean a private self-understanding or any kind of deep psychological or spiritual knowing of Self. Such a self-understanding is beyond the scope of this current inquiry, which is focusing on Dasein's Being-in-the-world. By

---

[62] Gelvin, 92.

[63] Heidegger's full quotation: "In so far as understanding and interpretation make up the existential state of Being of the 'there', 'meaning' must be conceived as the formal-existential framework of the disclosedness which belongs to understanding. Meaning is an existentiale of Dasein, not a property attaching to entities, lying 'behind' them, or floating somewhere as an 'intermediate domain'. Dasein only 'has' meaning, so far as the disclosedness of Being-in-the-world can be 'filled in' by the entities discoverable in that disclosedness. Hence only Dasein can be meaningful or meaningless" (151).

[64] Wrathall, Mark, *How to Read Heidegger*, New York, W.W. Norton, 2006, 41.

[65] I have avoided Heidegger's phrase "circumspective concern" because, fair or not, it strikes me as too suggestive of rational reflection.

"identity," then, I mean not any kind of inner knowing but the understanding of the relations that Dasein has with the world, which is related to Heidegger's discussion of "knowledge of Self"—Dasein's understanding of its Being-in-the-world throughout all constitutive items essential to it (146).

Because Dasein is Being-in-the-world, it necessarily has an understanding of its place and possibilities in the world, even if that understanding is without reflective intellectual content. Most individuals think of themselves in terms of their social acceptance or their material comforts while they are immersed in the everydayness of life. Dasein's identity exists not in and of itself but only as Dasein's relation to itself that is its response to itself within the world—the "I interacting with the world." The understanding that Dasein has of its place in the world is necessarily an interpretation—Dasein's own first-person evaluation of its role in the world that reflects its involvements. I agree with Blattner that "we are not just absorbed in the world, but our sense of identity, of who we are, cannot be disentangled from the world around us. We are what matters to us in our world."[66] Dasein's identity is proximally understood as a wholeness. Just as we proximally have in mind a tree, not a bundle of separate qualities, identity is a sense of wholeness, not a bundle of separate qualities. Just as we can, through reflection, break down the experience of a tree into separate qualities, we can break down our view of our identity into separate identity relations. These identity relations correspond to particular people, entities, times, and social constructions. In the broadest sense, an individual has an identity relation with every entity, person, and concept that exists because, if nothing else, there is potential for there to be involvement—my identity relation with someone I have never met is that I do not know him or her. When there is involvement, the identity relation has significance for the individual—I have no involvement with someone I do not even know exists.

Significance of identity relations can be forced onto an individual or chosen by him or her. For example, individuals have an identity relation with rules that they are compelled to live under, so those rules have a significance. Individuals have supervisors or other people in authority whom they must live and work under, and those bosses have significance. But that is different from the significance of a friend who is chosen. Even if the friend first appeared in one's life unbidden, the choice was made to allow that individual close as a

---

[66] Blattner, William, *Heidegger's Being and Time: A Reader's Guide*, New York, Continuum, 2006, 12.

friend. A boss may also be a friend, but "boss" and "friend" are different significances that may have difficulties in being reconciled—a workplace romance would be an even more complicated example. When we reflect on our identity relations, we can see that they are often complicated, multifaceted, and nuanced. Each identity relation is part of a constellation of intertwined and overlapping involvements in an individual that influences his or her identity.

The constellation of identity relations becomes even more complex when we add the existentiale that Dasein is always understanding itself in terms of its future possibilities (144-145). Included in every identity relation with every entity, person, and concept are the future possibilities for that identity relation. My identity relation with the person I have not met includes the possibility that I could meet him or her. With a friend, it includes the possibilities that they could help me or hurt me. All possibilities necessarily direct Dasein's attention toward the future, as all potentials actualize in the future. Thus, Dasein's identity is also a relation with its future, a relation that unfolds in Being-sphere as Dasein moves from being in one situation to being in the next by shifts in its readiness to interact with the world.

The public aspect of identity lies in the reality that identity is relational, defined by interaction with others, which is true on two levels. The first is definitional in that, for example, an individual cannot be a spouse without another person. The second is evaluative in that an individual being a good spouse is defined largely by those around the individual appraising the individual's actions in reference to social standards of what being a good spouse means. The individual, thus, is unavoidable dependent on others as the source of his or her identity and meaning. Primarily, an individual's identity is something that is learned from one's community and larger society. Most aspects of a person's identity are available to an individual only though the evaluations of other people. Individuals must depend on other people to show them what their identity relations are. From their first contact at birth with caregivers, individuals absorb the cues of the people around them as to how to be and who to be. Individuals respond within the possibilities for identity relations that are delineated by their social environment. The situation that identity is an essential part of an individual, yet the individual is dependent on others for that identity is a source of unease for the individual. How much interpersonal and social conflict is the result of this dependency and the friction and unease that it engenders? An individual's identity is a public affair, and this publicness pushes an individual to address issues of identity by looking more outward than inward.

The need for Dasein to include its relations with others in its identity pushes Dasein toward accommodation to, if not conformity with, other individuals and society. The need for accommodation to others includes the desire to be like others, what Heidegger terms "distantiality (126) but it also includes the pragmatic considerations that come from desiring to successfully complete one's projects in the world—we must accommodate other people and circumstances in the pursuit of our own ends. The pressure to conform reaches directly into Dasein's identity and Being-sphere, because Dasein's sees itself in terms of social pressure, but this pressure does not mean that Dasein has no identity without others. Dasein cannot help but be Dasein and cannot help but have an identity, but the particular components of that identity are the contingent, worldly identity relations of Dasein's life.

From what has been discussed so far, we can see how Being-sphere individuates people. Individuals, through their experiences and their responses to their experiences, each have their own distinct Being-spheres and develop their distinct constellations of meanings and of significances. And yes, Being-sphere is a bit crowded with constellations of identity relations, meanings, and significances. How I parse them out is that meanings are the intelligible as-somethings that Dasein holds,[67] significance is the involvements that Dasein holds, and identity relations are how Dasein understands entities and ideas as they relate to it. All of these components of Being-sphere interact with and contribute to how Dasein perceives and acts amidst the world.

The individual is not the source of public meaning or significance any more than the individual is the source of the world, but the individual acts within the world in an individuated way in response to the world. The individual does not create *the* world, the individual creates "*my* world"—the "true world" as mentioned earlier. That an individual's world is inseparable from and completely dependent on *the* world does not mean that it is not still that individual's world. This remains true regardless of how much or how little an

---

[67] Heidegger defines "meaning" as "*the 'upon-which' of a projection in terms of which something becomes intelligible as something*" (151, emphasis his). I find using the term "meaning" problematic, though, in that in normal language we also use the word as a synonym for "significance," as in "that holds meaning for me" and as a synonym for "definition," as in "the meaning of…" Both of these uses seem to both overlap and diverge from Heidegger's use of the term.

individual is aware of or introspective about his or her constellation of significances—the ontological character of individuation is inseparable from the individual. Being-sphere shows us that each individual person is a locus of significance. Dasein perceives and de-severs in terms not only of its involvements but also of how it perceives itself. Such bias is unavoidable. Understandably, an individual's sense of himself or herself and his or her involvements and projects are significant to him or her. It is, therefore, understandable that an individual will interpret events in terms of what is significant to him or her—all knowing is as-it-relates-to one's for-the-sake-of-whiches. All events in an individual's life are experienced in and interpreted through his or her identity because all experiences are experienced in Being-sphere, not a detached, objective space. In turn, the emphasis that significance brings to experience and responses affects an individual's Being-sphere.

How Dasein Encounters Entities in Being-sphere

We can now use Being-sphere to look at how Dasein functions in the world. First, we will look at how Being-sphere improves Heidegger's descriptions of how Dasein de-severs equipment and then move to how Being-sphere improves a description of human activity beyond physical objects.

Dasein is Being-in-the-world, which means that it dwells in a world in which it is both recipient and participant. Dasein comports itself to the world in using equipment to fulfill its personal involvements. But we must avoid thinking of this comportment in terms of a lingering Cartesian subject. It is misleading to think of regions as under the direction of a transcendental ego that arranges its world from on high. However, we must also avoid the opposite extreme. It is equally misleading to think of regions as a completely socially determined realm beyond the reach of an individual. Applying the concept of Being-sphere achieves a more balanced approach.

On one hand, an individual receives meaning from his or her society, and equipment use is a public endeavor. Equipment is perceived and used not just in terms of the individual's involvements but also in terms of "what humans can do." Primary to anyone's view of the world is what is possible for a person to do. When we look at any tool, the immediate understanding is "a person can use that." The thought "I can use that" is closely related but stems from the first. Brandom calls this a "responsive recognition" that is conducted in terms of the referential totality of significance that is the social lifeworld.[68] It is quite possible for an individual to be innovative in asking "what can *I* do with that?" but creativity is a movement beyond everydayness. There is a standard everyday social meaning of what a hammer is, and an individual receives that meaning from society. This standard meaning of equipment was not created by our age of mass production, but mass production has certainly enhanced this way of thinking.

On the other hand, the individual holds meaning for entities that is differentiated from public meaning. The interchangeable commoditization of equipment in our age has lessened but not eliminated an important question related to this: What makes an otherwise interchangeable entity take on personal meaning? There is a real difference between "a pen" and "my pen." A row of houses can be identical, but one of them is "my house." This significance is there even if we do not amend the entity with our personal touches; it is still perceived as "mine." This phenomenon can be explained only if we admit that an individual is not just a recipient of meaning but also a participant in meaning creation. "A pen" does not become "my pen" without the individual creating that possessive meaning. This meaning does not automatically happen when equipment is used. If I go to a store and choose a pen to buy, the economic and legal transaction makes the pen my property, but my placing significance on it being "my pen" is a separate act. Because equipment withdraws into the background (68), I could possess a pen for a long time and it may still hold no significance for me—I could use it transparently, and as long as it works it is invisible to me. Or I could bring it close to me as "my favorite pen," or any number of significances that distinguishes it from any other pen.

This dimension of de-severance is underappreciated by Heidegger and his commentators. This significance of something being "mine" resides not in the object or circumstances but in an individual's Being-sphere because significance does not float free—significance is held by Dasein, on either an individual or a social level. Significance does not necessarily transfer from social norms to an individual—the individual must engage in de-severance. Society can hold a

---

[68] Brandom, Robert, "Heidegger's Categories," Dreyfus, Hubert L. and Wrathall, Mark A. (eds.), *A Companion to Heidegger (Blackwell Companions to Philosophy),* Oxford, UK, Blackwell Publishers, 2005, 214-232. Brandom's overly complex and jargon-laden interpretation of social practice underplays the importance of individuated meaning and significance, instead arguing that communal recognition lies only in use of objects (p. 222), but his basic idea of responsive recognition is on target.

symbol in great esteem, yet there is no guarantee that an individual will take that relation of significance into his or her own Being-sphere, despite social pressure. Significance is held by an individual within his or her Being-sphere, and the totality of significances is part of what individuates Dasein.

Disentangling *Das Man* in Terms of Being-sphere

We can now apply the concept of Being-sphere more clearly to see and hope to correct Heidegger's portrayal of the individual Dasein oppressed by *das Man*[69] to show how Being-sphere can free Heideggerian notions for social and political theory. Heidegger focuses on the negative influence of *das Man*, calling it a "real dictatorship" (126) and identifying distantiality, averageness, and leveling down as ways that *das Man* controls how Dasein interprets itself and steals away from Dasein its independence, subjugating it under its dominion (127). Carman describes *das Man* as "Heidegger's anti-personification of the anonymous normativity that he thinks governs and in fact tyrannizes so much of Dasein's everyday understanding of itself and its world."[70] We must be careful not to turn *das Man* into a kind of bugbear. Heidegger misses several aspects of *das Man*. First, in overemphasizing the suppressive and mysterious qualities of *das Man*, he does not give proper place to the tangible practical effects of *das Man* in being a touchstone for social conduct. Second, he considers *das Man* as belonging to Dasein's constitution (129), a designation that prevents him from seeing how people act independently of *das Man* or how *das Man* itself is a product of social forces.

Heidegger's concept of *das Man* is important in describing Dasein's Being-in-the-world, but his conception has weaknesses. Yes, individuals are

---

[69] I will leave "*das Man*" untranslated. I agree with Dreyfus (Dreyfus, xi) that translating it to "the They" as Macquarrie and Robinson do, misleadingly suggests that we are not part of *das Man*. However, I do not think his alternative translation as "the one" sufficiently corrects this. I also think it too strongly suggests an active justification process of "what one does" rather than the background of norms that simply exists unbidden and unreflectively followed as Heidegger uses the term "*das Man*." Blattner's preferred translation, "The Anyone," more easily includes us, even suggests a desire to belong to it, and captures the anonymity of *das Man*. However, it lacks Heidegger's emphasis on the pressure it brings to our lives—what *das Man* delineates is not what "just anyone does"; it is what we are *supposed* to do.

[70] Carman, Taylor, "On Being Social: A Reply to Olafson." in *Inquiry*, 37:2 (1994), 213.

concerned about the ways they differ from others (126), but we need to distinguish between, on one hand, the general involuntary choices individuals make within the unreflective everydayness of Dasein's Being, and, on the other hand, choices that are genuinely coerced. To correct the picture, we must disentangle the forces that could be included within the concept of *das Man*. Society supplies a standard everyday social meaning that has both negative and positive consequences for individuals. As Schmid concludes, social norms and the public sphere play a positive and enabling role for our Being-in-the-world.[71] *Das Man* indicates the cultural force of the collective people in that time and space, the network of culturally constituted assignments of meanings and equipment. Wittgenstein's forms of life have some connections with Heidegger's *das Man*. Wittgenstein's concern was language and meaning, but I believe his ideas of a social sphere that provides individuals with rules of language and meaning connect with the notion of Being-sphere.[72] Language is learned from society, which teaches the individual the appropriate and inappropriate uses of words and grammar, which is basically how all social norms are learned.

It is true that people appear to concern themselves with what most people concern themselves with, but we must not assume that all such sameness is the result of coercive social pressure. We concern ourselves with food and our identity not because society tells us to but because they are necessary features of, respectively, staying alive and being Dasein. How and what we eat and how we determine our identity is from *das Man*, but the initial impulses are not. Concern and knowing are existentialia to which ontic considerations are attached. This extends to knowledge in general: Although we learn what trees are from society, it should come as no surprise that we also learn about trees from the reality of the trees that is experienced by us.

What the force of *das Man* does is channel impetuses in certain ways by providing a structure. But again, this structure is not necessarily in opposition to individual involvements; it could reflect general best practices. Kosher food rules are strict but serve a purpose of reducing food-borne diseases. A society

---

[71] Schmid, Hans Bernhard, "The Broken We," in *Tonoc*, 2:11, 2005, 16-27; 18.

[72] Olafson accuses Dreyfus of assimilating Heidegger's account of human being to the later-Wittgenstein's theory of language as rule governed (Olafson, Frederick A., "Heidegger a'la Wittgenstein or 'Coping' with Professor Dreyfus," in *Inquiry*, 37:1, 1994, 46). Olafson may have a point about Dreyfus, but I do not agree with his claim that there are no significant affinities between Heidegger and Wittgenstein.

builds houses in a certain way that works within that climate. Everydayness, thus, does not indicate the best way of doing things but a way of doing things that has worked in the past sufficiently well that it continues to be the normal way of doing things currently. It also does not mean that it continues to work well, because everydayness can be the expression of a tradition that has ceased to be useful, but the impetus of its normal everydayness drives its continued use.

I am inclined to think that *das Man* is as Theodore Schatzki suggests: a public space in which people encounter each other.[73] With this interpretation, we can also consider Olafson's suggestion that "[*Das Man*] could simply be a distorted modality of Mitsein in which we all systematically detour around one another and ourselves in our authentic capacity as Dasein."[74] We can see individuals as immersed in a public space in which they coexist with other individuals and *das Man* is present but not all powerful. Still, as Schatzki observes, Heidegger does not solve the problem of the relation between an individual Dasein and the larger social world. Schatzki notes that Dreyfus contends that the concept of *das Man* solves the above-mentioned problem because *das Man* socializes individuals into the shared social world.[75] This concept fits with Dreyfus's conception of *das Man* as a positive force for teaching meaning and practice, but it only explains learning social skills and does not explain individual responses to society outside of adherence to social norms. A society can say, "this is what it makes sense to do," but that expression of a norm is not sufficient to compel an individual to act. *Das Man* provides acceptable possibilities to individuals, but it does not provide all possibilities for individuals, a fact that Schatzki acknowledges.[76] Dreyfus's solution also does not explain differences in individual experiences and beliefs. Although it is true that individuals mostly experience the world in the same ways, it is not true that they *always* experience the world in the same ways. Nor does Dreyfus's solution explain how individuals interact with each other; it instead reduces social interaction to training in and compliance with a hegemony of social norms.

The weaknesses in Heidegger's conception of *das Man* are resolved by the concept of Being-sphere. I side with Schatzki's conclusion: "For the

---

73 Schatzki, Theodore R. "Early Heidegger on Sociality," Dreyfus, Hubert L. and Wrathall, Mark A. (eds.), *A Companion to Heidegger (Blackwell Companions to Philosophy)*, Oxford, UK, Blackwell Publishers, 2005, 239-240.
74 Olafson, 59.
75 Schatzki, 240 and Dreyfus, 145.
76 Schatzki, 244.

purposes of social ontology, Heidegger's account would have to be rounded out by a richer analysis of the modes of coexistence."[77] Being-sphere is the hermeneutical tool with which we can develop such an analysis because Being-sphere is the nexus of individual practice by which individuals interact with their world. By stressing the individual as engaged agent, we can better balance Heidegger's contention that *das Man* is the central ontology of the everyday Mitsein with Olafson's observation that *das Man* is the "anonymous and undifferentiated mode of being that accrues to each of us on certain occasions and for *certain purposes*."[78] Individuals *do* have occasions and purposes independent of *das Man* because they are engaged agents with concernful involvements. Not even all of everydayness is the averageness and leveling down of *das Man* but includes individuals' natural impulses such as the desire for food as discussed earlier. Also, though it is correct to say that different Dasein are in-one-and-the-same-world, which Schatzki equates with *das Man*,[79] it is also correct to say that different Dasein are in that same world as distinct Being-spheres. Even in everydayness, each Dasein is individuated by its Being-sphere, which encompasses its particular experiences and responses. Being-sphere is *how* Dasein is *there*.

Heidegger speaks briefly about a "constancy" that is "Dasein's kind of Being as Being-with [other people]" (128). Although he interprets this constancy as an "inauthenticity and failure to stand by one's Self" (128), we would do well to be more phenomenological about this constancy of everyday Being-with-others. The proximal character of Dasein's interaction with the world is everydayness. Heidegger's everydayness is a mode of Being that is a kind of leveling down, but the question is why. Seeing Being-sphere as a state of Being shows us. In everydayness, individuals deal with the world and with others with an economy of thinking. This is the pragmatic impulse to simplify the complexities of life. It is, for example, quicker and easier to know people, even ourselves, by identities according to social roles rather than as individuals.[80] Thus, we hold people, including ourselves, in our Being-sphere as identities, and these held identities serve as a shortcut. Expedient identities become true for us

---

[77] Schatzki, 246.
[78] Olafson, 56 (emphasis mine).
[79] Schatzki, 239.
[80] Mulhall considers assigning identities to other people according to social roles our normal way of dealing with Others, 72.

in our everyday lives.[81] As William James said, truth is "only the expedient in the way of our thinking, just as the right is only the expedient in the way of our behaving." It is never the case that individuals act without holding identities about entities, but it is usually the case that these held identities are unexamined. In everyday life, much expediency is because so many of life's activities have already been worked out for individuals. If one needs to dig a hole, one does not need to invent equipment to accomplish that goal; society has already invented the shovel. One knows how to live and carry on the basic functions of life, at least by adulthood.

But is there still individuation in the face of *das Man*? Yes, because in its Being-sphere, Dasein interacts with the world, and comports to it in terms of its involvements. Everydayness does not imply that Dasein is doing nothing in response. Experiences engender responses, and Dasein is continually responding to the world in its Being-sphere. Even blindly following the crowd is a response. Predominantly, Dasein's responses are without reflection and are just reactions, sometimes referred to as "emotional reactions," or as "following the crowd." Everyday responses such as repulsion or attraction are states of existence because they require no mental content (141). Encountering something as threatening is a kind of intentionality, but it requires no reflection; reflection would be additional and not required for us to able to respond.[82] A response that stems from reflection would be a reply, not a reaction, which is a possibility, but not the proximal way that Dasein responds to the world. An individual can pause and consider his or her circumstances and possibilities and make a reply based on those considerations. These are not necessarily rational decisions—the considerations could be entirely irrational—nevertheless, reflection has happened. When an individual remains in everydayness, he or she is reacting, despite the passivity.

Individuals tend to choose the well-worn paths, and not without merit. We can apply a notion of custom or habit as second nature for coping with the world, what Davis calls a "nonwilling corresponding"[83] or what Dreyfus calls "transparent coping."[84] Habit works on two levels, and both are part of the

[81] James, William, "Pragmatism's Conception of Truth," Thayer, H.S. (ed.), *Pragmatism: The Classic Writings*, New York, Hackett Publishing, 1982, 238.
[82] Dreyfus, 175.
[83] Davis, Bret W., "Introduction: Key Concepts in Heidegger's Thinking of Being," Davis, Bret W. (ed.), *Martin Heidegger: Key Concepts,* Durham, UK, Acumen, 2010, 13.

constellation of significance in Being-sphere. There is the practical level at which we use equipment, such as operating a light switch or believing that stopping at red lights is a good practice. At this level, individuals follow *das Man* to understand how to function constructively in the world. An individual strives to actualize his or her possibilities and seize the practical possibilities of entities he or she encounters by enowning practical meanings.[85] Then there is a level of narratives to explain how the world works, such as "honesty is the best policy," "America is the greatest country on Earth," or "dialectical materialism explains human history." Such narratives, when de-severed into significance, are held by an individual as explanations of the world and give the individual a feeling of control over events and circumstances. Public norms are often de-severed without reflection but in everydayness but still become narratives of "what one does." Beliefs become the basis for action, become ingrained as habits, and are held as identities in the Being-sphere.

Strongly held beliefs or narratives become so ingrained in an individual Dasein's Being-sphere that they take on a basic existential-ontological "there." By this, I mean that a belief or narrative can become what I will call a "framework narrative," meaning that it provides a foundation for held identities either of self or of something else. For example, "I am worthless" or "all gypsies are thieves" can be more than propositions; they can be held identities that are frameworks for comportments toward the world. When an individual's experiences touch on, for example, the self, if one's strongly held identity for oneself is "I am worthless," then this framework narrative is the basic existential way in which the individual is his or her existential "there" in the world. I purposely borrow Heidegger's language to describe *Befindlichkeit* because, as I will argue shortly, the moods of *Befindlichkeit* also come from Dasein's own dispositions. Strongly held identities like "I am worthless" existentially deliver Dasein over to the character of the identity. Heidegger might reply that I am confusing Dasein's belief about its whither with the "that-it-is" of its "there" (136), the "there" being Dasein's "thrownness," the facticity of being delivered over to the world. I will address that shortly, but for now, I am suggesting that

---

[84] Dreyfus, 147.

[85] Boedeker Jr., Edgar C., "Individual and Community in Early Heidegger: Situating *Das Man*, the Man-Self, and Self-Ownership in Dasein's Ontological Structure," in *Inquiry*, 44:1, 2001, 63-99. Similar is Schmid's term, "practical intentionality," which is not a matter of cognition but of "practical everyday coping," Schmid, 17.

framework narratives like "I am worthless" are beliefs about its whither that are existentially present in Dasein's Being-sphere in the same way as are the moods of *Befindlichkeit*. Acknowledging this, we have an insight into a wide range of phenomena of individual responses to the world, from conformity to *das Man*, to racism, and what Heidegger calls "moods." That individuals would come, over the course of life, to a distinct set of beliefs and narratives contributes to why they act in distinctly individual ways.

When a belief held by an individual is challenged, that individual feels unease—as described by American pragmatists such as C. S. Pierce—that compels the individual to either alter or entrench his or her beliefs because of fear of a loss of control over events and circumstances. The depth and character of the unease are relative to the level of the belief challenged. At the level of framework narratives, a challenge can be deeply threatening. Such challenges have a significant role to play in why individuals cling to identities and narratives that are social pathologies such as racist or nationalist narratives of superiority. The desire for a belief that explains the world explains why people will cling to identities and narratives even in the face of contrary evidence. Any such identities and narratives are part of an individual Dasein's Being-sphere and affect its perceptions and comportments.

This discussion of the desirability of identities and narratives provides an additional explanation for how individuals respond to the realities of *das Man*. Individuals have the freedom to act in different ways, but they have motive to act in ways that benefit themselves, and acting within social norms is often to their benefit. Thus, individuals receive a return on their investment in beliefs; even if that return is falsely perceived by the individual, the individual believes it is there. The force of everydayness is not the only cause of an individual conforming to social norms. Heidegger's discussion of distantiality focuses too much on the negative reaction to peer pressure, which is part of his distorted picture of what *das Man* provides. Yes, there is the real human fear of not fitting in, but social mores of style and behavior are only a part of the norms of society. With Being-sphere, we can see that Dasein has leeway to respond according to its own involvements and beliefs.

Being-sphere and *Befindlichkeit*

Being-sphere improves Heidegger's ontological concept of *Befindlichkeit*,[86] which ontically are our moods (134). *Befindlichkeit* is the state in which we find ourselves, and *Stimmung* (moods) reflects an ontic attunement to the state in which we find ourselves (134). I will discuss some problems with the basic concept of *Befindlichkeit* and then how Being-sphere helps resolve them. My argument is not against the concept of *Befindlichkeit* itself but that Heidegger's conception of it is incomplete.

Heidegger calls *Befindlichkeit* a "basic existential way in which Dasein is its 'there'" (135, 139) that "implies a disclosive submission to the world, out of which we can encounter something that matters to us" (137).[87] What does this mean? Dasein's Being is always an issue for it, so when would nothing matter for Dasein? Would a situation in which nothing matters to Dasein be a lack of mood?[88] But Heidegger says "that in every case Dasein always has some mood…[and] is always disclosed moodwise" (134), and this is consistent with the overall view he presents of Dasein as "always somehow directed and on its way" (79) and always familiar with significance (87). So, if *Befindlichkeit* does not make mattering itself possible, it seems that Heidegger means that moods are the means by which what matters is disclosed to Dasein; that encountering what matters "is grounded in one's *Befindlichkeit*" (137). It seems that Heidegger holds that *Befindlichkeit* is the only means by which what matters to us is disclosed to us.[89]

---

[86] I will leave *Befindlichkeit* untranslated. Macquarrie and Robinson's translation, "state of mind," is, as Mulhall says, "seriously misleading," Mulhall, 76.

[87] Dreyfus states that *Befindlichkeit* "conveys being found in a situation where things and options already matter," Dreyfus, 168.

[88] Heidegger does speak of a "lack of mood" but explains that in it "Being has become manifest as a burden" (134).

[89] Heidegger expresses this multiple times: *"The mood has already disclosed, in every case, Being-in-the-world as a whole, and makes it possible first of all to direct oneself towards something"* (137, emphasis his). "Dasein's openness to the world is constituted existentially by the attunement of [*Befindlichkeit*]" (137). "Under the strongest pressure and resistance, nothing like an affect would come about, and the resistance itself would remain essentially undiscovered, if Being-in-the-world, with its [*Befindlichkeit*], had not already submitted itself to having entities within-the-world 'matter' to it in a way which its moods have outlined in advance" (137). And "In *fearing as such,* what we have thus characterized as threatening is freed and allowed to matter to us (141, emphasis his).

A mood discloses our facticity, the situation in which we find ourselves, which is, Heidegger says, "Dasein in its thrownness and its submission to that world which is already disclosed with its own Being" (139). The translations for *Befindlichkeit* preferred by Dreyfus, "affectedness,"[90] and Blattner, "affectivity,"[91] are true to Heidegger's sense of how Dasein is passive in how Dasein finds itself in the world. Heidegger sees Dasein as delivered over in its mood to the world much in the same way that Dasein is subjugated by *das Man*, diminishing if not eliminating any leeway for individuation. Heidegger's *Befindlichkeit* is an existential submission to the world (137) in which Dasein is delivered over (135), and *Befindlichkeit* discloses Dasein's submission to the world (139). Heidegger's example of *Befindlichkeit* is the mood of fear. Heidegger's position seems to be that in fear one is always given over to it. He calls fear a bewilderment[92] in which Dasein "forgets itself and therefore does not take hold of any definite possibility" (342). And this is true of not just fear but all "bad moods": "In these, Dasein becomes blind to itself, the environment with which it is concerned veils itself, the circumspection of concern gets led astray" (136). Even good moods such as "hope, joy, enthusiasm, [and] gaiety," Heidegger says, must be analyzed no differently than bad moods (345). All moods and *Befindlichkeit,* he says, disclose Dasein in its thrownness (136, 139), which he defines as the *a priori* state of Dasein being determined by and submissive to circumstances outside its control (139). Although thrownness does not preclude positive circumstances, Heidegger gives us little sense of it being anything but negative. Heidegger's position fits with his view of *das Man* as an external negative presence.[93]

What, though, do moods disclose? Wrathall, true to Heidegger's descriptions of fear and the etymology of "mood" as "attunement,"[94] says that "the fear I feel…shows me *how I stand* with respect to the world around me—it shows me *how I am* vulnerable in relation to what is threatening me."[95] That

---

[90] Dreyfus, 168-169.

[91] Blattner, William, "Temporality," *Blackwell Companion to Heidegger*, Malden, MA, Blackwell Publishing, 2005, 311-324; 312.

[92] "Fear discloses Dasein predominantly in a privative way. It bewilders us and makes us 'lose our heads'" (141).

[93] "Ontologically, we thus obtain as the *first* essential characteristic of *[Befindlichkeit]*— that *they disclose Dasein in its thrownness, and-proximally and for the most part-in the manner of an evasive turning-away"* (136, emphasis his).

[94] Macquarrie and Robinson in *Being and Time*, 172, fn. 3.

would be a true statement if moods were always an accurate representation of the world around one. Wrathall's example of fear is hearing footsteps behind one in a darkened alley,[96] but though most people can associate such a situation with a mood of fear, does fear accurately show how one stands in relation to the situation? To use another example, does a person afraid of spiders actually stand vulnerable in relation to spiders? Clearly not; a mood alters only the individual's perception. Wittgenstein observed that "the world of the happy man is a different one from that of the unhappy man" and that though an exercise of the will does not alter facts in the world, it does alter the sense one has of it.[97] Heidegger agrees that a mood like fear does not disclose a brute fact about the world but an existential "there" (135). The "there" that *Befindlichkeit* discloses is not the external world but Dasein's "true world" of Being-sphere. Similarly, Dreyfus says that *Befindlichkeit* is not of the structure of the world but is a structure of Dasein's Being-in-the-world [98]; however, as we have seen, the existential where of Dasein's Being-in-the-world and its involvements is Being-sphere. Because *Befindlichkeit* is not what makes mattering possible but is the means by which what matters to us is disclosed to us, then the existential where of *Befindlichkeit* is Being-sphere. Because of differences in experiences, the Being-sphere of one individual *is* different from another's, and this difference contributes to differences in perception and responses for different individuals and differences in what matters to an individual. When we fear, Heidegger says, we are encountering something that "has detrimentality as its kind of involvement," a definite involvement within a context of involvements (140). But involvements are individuated in Dasein's distinct Being-sphere. Thus, what moods reveal is Dasein's distinct Being-sphere.

What Heidegger calls "mood" is best understood as an aspect of Being-sphere. It arises out of and is part of the structure of Dasein's Being-in-the-world (136). All of Dasein's *Befindlichkeit* existentially reside in Being-sphere in a similar way as do Dasein's knowing and comportment. Dreyfus says that *Befindlichkeit* is neither a feeling nor a comportment but a "component of the activity of clearing."[99] Dreyfus's observation is in keeping with Being-sphere as

---

95 Wrathall, *How to Read Heidegger*, 34 (emphasis mine).
96 Wrathall, *How to Read Heidegger*, 33.
97 Wittgenstein, proposition 6.43.
98 Dreyfus, 170.
99 Dreyfus, 173.

the clearing of Dasein's Being-in-the-world. Moods are existentially within Being-sphere because they have the same inside-outside structure as does knowing. Wrathall explains that the mood of fear is not inside ("the fear in the alleyway does not come from me"), nor is it from outside ("the alleyway isn't objectively fearful").[100] Moods are experienced inside by Dasein and are also publically shared with others, Wrathall says, and moods are affected by an individual's social world, Mulhall says,[101] so it would seem that a mood is something both inside and outside Dasein, which places moods within Being-sphere. A mood, when present, is an existential happening in Being-sphere that Dasein can comport to or not depending on its involvements. In this way, moods are akin to knowing. When we learn something, it changes how we perceive things because what we have learned previously flavors our current and future perceptions. Similarly, our moods color our perceptions of things (Wrathall gives the excellent example of how when we are bored everything has a flavor of being boring.[102]) A mood, like a knowing, could have enough force to compel Dasein to act, but Heidegger's example of fear is an unfortunate representation of moods because of the extreme nature that fear can take that many other moods do not. Moods like fear, grief, and rage can rise to the level of making us "lose our heads" (141), but most moods, like boredom, do not.

Adopting the concept of Being-sphere we can see that a mood is but one element among others that discloses how we find ourselves, which will better reflect the phenomena we see in individuals. We find our state and our possibilities not in a mood alone but in the dynamic of our experiences, involvements, and comportments. Yes, as Dreyfus and Wrathall say, "our moods govern and structure our comportment,"[103] but our comportments also affect our moods. Being in a hurry is a comportment that could become a mood that discloses our situation. We become blasé or cynical, jaded or confused, through a series of experiences and responses to them that contribute to moods and become dispositions. Although a mood cannot be willed, moods include attitudes that well up within Being-sphere.

For example, through thinking about things in particular ways one can bring oneself to a state of fear. If we normally walk a particular route each day,

---

[100] Wrathall, *How to Read Heidegger*, 34.
[101] Mulhall, 79
[102] Wrathall, *How to Read Heidegger*, 36.
[103] Dreyfus and Wrathall, 5.

then hear that someone was mugged on that route, we start to worry. That worry could, depending on our involvements, progress to fear. Not every individual would fear, because each individual has a distinct set of experiences, involvements, identities, and comportments, but Heidegger's conception does not seem to allow for these differences. If we let a mouse loose in a room full of people, some would laugh, some would be disturbed, a few would be frightened. What concept can explain that individuals differ in their responses to events? *Befindlichkeit* cannot, nor can *das Man*, because both focus too much on the passivity of individuals in the face of *Befindlichkeit* and *das Man*. If we see Dasein as entering all situations neither as a mechanistic object nor as a bare subject but as Being-sphere already laden with its knowings and involvements, we then see a mood as an aspect of Being-sphere through which Dasein can relate to the situation. If an individual has become fearful in his or her disposition, that individual is more prone to respond to a particular situation in the mood of fear.

When we see moods as existentially residing in Being-sphere, we can better see how they fit into Dasein's responses to its environment. I touched on responses earlier in how Dasein can, without reflection, react, or with reflection, reply. All moods, when present, are experienced as part of Dasein's interaction with the world to which Dasein responds in terms of its involvements. When a mood is strong, it assails us, we are given over to it, and we react out of that mood. But not all moods are so strong that they assail us, and we have leeway to respond. We may be bored at work, but we can fight through it and do our job. We can feel the fear and do a task anyway.[104] Returning briefly to our earlier discussion of strongly held identities, we can see how they have similar phenomena. When an identity like "I am worthless," is strong enough, it assails us, we are given over to it, and we react out of that belief; but we also can feel that mood of worthlessness (for it can manifest as what most people would call a mood) and fight through it and do a task anyway. The point is that combining Heidegger's insights on *Befindlichkeit* with Dasein's Being-sphere provides a broader conception of Dasein and its projection into its possibilities.

---

[104] Heidegger's brief acknowledgement that we can "master" our moods (136) is unconvincing, being almost a parenthetical aside absent in his later discussion.

How Dasein Encounters Others in Being-sphere

How Dasein encounters other people in terms of Being-sphere is a huge, complex topic requiring considerable explanation, but some introductory comments are in order. Dasein is always dynamically interacting with its environment, including other people, and is thus ontologically predisposed to Being-with, even when one is alone (120).[105] Dasein comports itself always toward a shared public world—the world *is* a world of Dasein (118). Heidegger calls them "Others"[106] not in opposition to Dasein but in similarity—they are other Dasein like us. These Others have a far more profound effect on us than do entities. We have, in fact, "a sort of reciprocity" that reigns between us and Others.[107] Most of our actions involve other people, what we work on is provided to us by Others, and our work is intended for Others (117). We understand Others as Dasein-with pursuing projects in the same way that we are, and those Others understand us as Dasein-with (121); even the attempt to understand oneself is grounded in Dasein-with (124), as I discussed earlier concerning identity.

An individual's Being-sphere is structured largely in terms of Being-with Others. Being-in-the-world means that our involvements relate to Others and their involvements. Heidegger's examples of the tended field, the tailored

---

[105] Sartre's criticism of Heidegger on this point shows that Sartre misunderstands. Heidegger says: "Our task is to make visible phenomenally the species to which this Dasein-with in closest everydayness belongs" (116). Thus, what Heidegger is describing in Being-with is the phenomenology of Dasein's everydayness. The everyday world of Dasein is a with-world, as he states: "This 'with' is something of the character of Dasein; the 'too' means a sameness of Being as circumspectively concerned Being-in-the-world. 'With' and 'too' are to be understood *existentially,* not categorically. By reason of this *with-like* Being-in-the-world, the world is always the one that I share with Others. The world of Dasein is a *with-world.* Being-in is *Being-with* Others. Their Being-in-themselves within-the-world is *Dasein-with*" (118, emphasis his). Sartre's contention that Heidegger's preexisting category of anonymous Being-with precludes the ability to have a genuine encounter with a particular person is a fallacy of division. What is true of universal everyday Being-in-the-world cannot be assumed to be true of particular encounters with other individuals who could be encountered in the comportment of everydayness or something more concrete and personal. Sartre, Jean-Paul, *Being and Nothingness: An Essay on Phenomenological Ontology*, Barnes, Hazel E. (tr.), New York, Simon & Schuster, 1956, 333-334.

[106] I will keep Macquarrie and Robinson's capitalization and use "Other" strictly in the Heideggerian sense.

[107] Schatzki, 238.

clothes, the book from a store, and the discovered boat all speak to ways in which we interact and share the world with Others (117-118). His examples show that Dasein's Being-with is true even when no one else is present. In the examples of the field and the boat, the owners of those entities need not be anywhere around for us to understand that they exist. In the book example, the bookstore owner need not continue to be present for us to understand that the book in our possession was once in the bookstore owner's possession. If we are tailoring an item of clothing, the person need not be present for us to understand that the work we are doing is intended for another. In all of these understandings, we are aware not only of our own concerns but also of the concerns of Others—that these are not mere objects but a part of someone else's world (117-118). Our interactions with Others are guided by our understanding of Others as Dasein like ourselves; we (usually) respect the fact that they are real people with real concerns.

Interaction with Others is proximally in terms of Being-sphere in two ways: one, because Dasein de-severs Others in the same way it de-severs equipment; and two, because interpersonal encounters are proximally in everydayness and between the public faces of Being-sphere. I will discuss each in turn.

We encounter Others as participants in the world of our involvements, so our encounters with them are always understood in regard to our involvements. Other individuals stand out from the nonhuman background, and we respond to them in terms of our identity relations with them, our past experiences, our current feelings and judgments about them, the time and place of the encounter, and our other concerns at the time. If we are lost in thought, we may be unaware of the person, and he or she does not enter into our significance. If we are concerned for our safety, the other person may be perceived as a threat and an intrusion into our significance, and we are disturbed. If we have no involvements, then we think no more than that there is another person passing by. But if we know the person, then the encounter is "lit up" in our significance. Heidegger speaks of equipment and the context of equipment being "lit up" in the modes of concern (72-75) and, because Others are also part of Dasein's involvements, it makes perfect sense to say that Others can be "lit up" in the modes of concern. Heidegger's use of "lit up" is in regard to equipment ready-to-hand, and he states that Others "are neither present-at-hand nor ready-to-hand" (118), but because Others are also "encountered from out of the world" (119), it stands to reason that Others would also be "lit up."

Because Being-sphere is how Dasein is Being-in-the-world, everydayness characterizes how Dasein proximally interacts with the world. Most of our responses to Others lie in the everyday, the impersonal. Individuals see each other only in terms of their own involvements and social roles: the clerk at the store is just that—his or her identity is as a clerk not an individual,[108] and the impersonal everydayness is strengthened. Everydayness is a mode of Being in Dasein; it is not just perception, but Dasein's perceptions of Others are colored by the mode of being of the everydayness of Being-sphere. In our everydayness, we keep Others outside of significance. Heidegger says that "listening to ... is Dasein's existential way of Being-open as Being-with for Others" (163). But "listening to ..." is not proximal, and Being-open with others is not proximal—everydayness is. Listening to and Being-open are modes of Being that Dasein must choose to enter—these modes are not proximal, nor can they be coerced; we can yell at someone, but we cannot make him or her take in our words.

Dasein gives an intimate reply only after a boundary of significance has been allowed to be crossed and the other person has been brought close and considered. The boundary of significance that delineates de-severing another person from the crowd and into intimacy is perhaps impossible to define, but it is one of the most significant aspects of human life. Bringing someone close past the boundary of significance into intimacy is an individual choice that cannot be coerced. An individual's physical and emotional boundaries can be violated, but an individual cannot be forced to feel intimately about another. The bringing close into significance of another alters the individual's Being-sphere and his or her involvements. In our bringing others close, their concerns become our concerns beyond the general human respect that we accord Others in everydayness. Bringing another person close extends into moral considerations—we do not accord strangers the same moral value that we do those with whom we are intimate. Such moral differences are highly variable and open up a huge new topic for future inquiry. But for now, I observe that

---

[108] Mulhall: "Their identity is thus given primarily by their occupation, by the tasks or functions they perform; who they are to us is a matter of what they do and how they do it. But these are defined purely impersonally, by reference to what the relevant task or office requires; given the necessary competence, which individual occupies that office is as irrelevant as are any idiosyncrasies of character and talent which have no bearing on the task at hand." 72.

such de-severances of Others are part of what individuates Dasein in its Being-sphere.

Ontologically, because the individual is proximally in everydayness, an individual seldom actually encounters or interacts with another individual. Instead, one's Being-sphere temporarily and marginally intersects and interacts with the publicness of the Being-spheres of other Dasein. Individuals experience each other proximally in everydayness not in intimacy, and, thus, Others are kept at a distance in terms of significance. To continue Heidegger's example of "listening to…," we can say that two individuals are "not hearing each other" or are "talking past each other." Interactions in everydayness, the absence of intimate contact with other people, leads to the response that society is impersonal and in turn leads to the concept of *das Man*. Everyday life is impersonal; we "put on a public face" in public space. Only when a state of familiarity and comfort has been reached do people interact with each other beyond everydayness. A different mode of being is entered into, and Being-spheres intersect in an intimate way. Heidegger makes one brief mention of this phenomenon of people connecting "deeper" than everydayness when Dasein "devote themselves to the same affair in common," when they can, if they take hold of their Dasein each in their own way, become *"authentically*[109] bound together" (122). But he does not pursue this idea or explain what sort of taking hold of their Dasein would bind two Dasein together. Being-sphere offers an answer: When two individuals share a particular significance in a particular now, de-sever the other in terms of significance, and mutually acknowledge this, they move "deeper" than everydayness and co-constitute a shared space of intimacy. Unless both individuals share these aspects of their current experience, the encounter is not personal and remains impersonal.

Another factor contributing to a lack of direct interpersonal encounters is that an individual's understandings and comportments influence how he or she experiences his or her environment. There is a human tendency to encounter things not in terms of how they are but in terms of how a person wants them to be in accordance with his or her involvements. This bias is a way of being that

---

[109] Emphasis his. I am scrupulously avoiding the massive and complicated topic of authenticity-inauthenticity because Heidegger states that everydayness is *a priori* to authenticity-inauthenticity (44). I situate Being-sphere similarly in relation to authenticity-inauthenticity and have room in this essay for only the existential structure of Being-sphere.

manifests in the perceptual comportment of Being-sphere. When Dasein experiences Others, they are either brought close, or not, and placed within Dasein's Being-sphere in terms of its involvements. The other person becomes connected with an identity that Dasein holds in its Being-sphere reflecting how that other person intersects with Dasein's involvements. In future interactions with the other person, Dasein perceives not entirely the other person but the identity Dasein holds of the other person.

Holding an identity leads to Dasein perceiving a person differently from how the other person would perceive himself or herself. Held identities work both ways. It is inevitable that Dasein will encounter Others who respond to it not in terms of how it sees itself but in terms of Others' identity for it. This discrepancy can be jarring because issues of personal identity have deep and profound effects on individuals and can spark strong responses from them. More widespread is that the disconnection of identities contributes to the impersonal everydayness of society. Each individual enters into the common social space not as a Cartesian subject but as his or her distinct Being-sphere and its distinct involvements and identities through which it perceives the world. But individual bias is only half of the situation. Being-sphere is not transparent; no one can see in to observe an individual's de-severences, significances, moods, or dispositions, only the individual's responses that manifest in observable physical actions. Individuals interact not with other individuals but with the public face of Others' distinct Being-spheres. Such publicness, absent of a de-severance into intimacy, is the impersonal character of everyday interaction.

Being-sphere accommodates these phenomena of impersonal and intimate relations, indifference, friendship, and romance because it gives weight to the importance of how Dasein as an engaged agent is situated in the world as an entity that has concernful involvements in which it projects itself into the world in terms of its involvements and projects. These involvements in turn alter its mode of Being, perceptions, and actions. Held identities alter Dasein's perceptions of facts so that they meaningfully alter Dasein's relation to the world, which leads us back to the primacy of Being-sphere in social relations. In *das Man* are the collective identities of society—how society sees itself.[110] When an individual experiences the diffuse but ever present *das Man*, he or she is being affected by, assessed in terms of, and forced to respond to those

---

[110] In this, perhaps Dreyfus has a point about *das Man* being a substitute Dasein, Dreyfus, 158-159.

identities. *Das Man*, if anything, is an idea within Being-sphere, a belief or framework narrative about what "they" are doing, thinking, and feeling and how one should respond. This is not to suggest that society and its institutions do not exert power on individuals, but if that power is exerted directly, it is done so through individuals and received by individuals. The indirect power of society and its institutions flows through the collective social environment shared by individuals. Being-sphere clarifies these relations by bringing to the fore the structure of Dasein's Being-in-the-world as a distinct entity with distinct constellations of identity relations, meanings, and significances.

Conclusions and Future Research

Being-sphere opens a hermeneutic for social and political theory by seeing interpersonal relations as a dynamic interaction of individual Being-spheres. This interpretation avoids the extreme of an isolated Cartesian subject because we are not trying to explain how multiple subjective inner spheres are interacting. We are instead explaining how distinct Being-spheres, each one formed through actively interacting with the world, are responding to each other. We then begin not from detached people but involved people.[111] The Being-sphere concept does not push the interaction problem to another level because it recognizes that interaction is what forms and structures Dasein's Being-in-the-world. Being-sphere incorporates the equiprimordial foundation of Dasein and Dasein's Being-in-the-world, and that interaction with other Dasein is inherent in the public world.

Being-sphere also avoids the other extreme of beginning without individuals at all and attempting to explain society in terms of forces or transcendental structures. Being-sphere does not reduce away the individual but acknowledges his or her place in responding to and constructing society. Dasein, when it comports itself toward the world, is not detached from or absent from the world but contributes to and is involved in a shared world. There are as many Being-spheres as there are individuals. Each Being-sphere, being the dynamic interaction of an individual with the world, is overlapping with other Being-spheres. The private remains out of reach, but

---

[111] Being-sphere also has the fortunate corollary of avoiding splitting the world into two separate realms—the "real" and the sensual.

physical space, time, involvements, significances, and goals are shared—not internally, but outside in Being-sphere; not outside separate from Dasein, but inside Being-sphere.[112]

Further phenomenological analysis of Being-sphere needs to include how Being-spheres interact in common space to create publicness. It also needs to take into account the significant distinctions between how individuals perceive other people as same versus as Other, because these distinctions, manifested in Being-sphere, are significant in ethical and social questions. Another issue is how Being-sphere can explain the hegemony of power as a structure that is found in all attempts at empowerment and oppression, and not only at a social level. Further analysis also needs to explain how identities are projected by individuals onto other individuals, rendering the Other as reduced to that identity. Finally, Being-sphere needs to explain phenomena such as racialized space—space created by people, structured by their system of involvements, that projects prejudiced identities onto other individuals. I believe that Being-sphere has the hope of addressing these social phenomena in ways that previous theories cannot.

---

[112] Dreyfus has a similar formulation when he writes: "[T]he world is the whole of which all subworlds are elaborations. Now we add that subworlds are lived in by a particular Dasein by being-in-a-situation. Each Dasein's there is the situation as organized around its activity. The shared situation is called the clearing, being-in-the-clearing is being-there," Dreyfus, 165.

Bibliography

Blattner, William. "Existence and Self-Understanding in *Being and Time*." *Philosophy and Phenomenological Research 56* (1996).

Blattner, William, *Heidegger's Being and Time: A Reader's Guide*, New York, Continuum, 2006.

Blattner, William, "Temporality," Dreyfus, Hubert L. and Wrathall, Mark A. (eds.), *A Companion to Heidegger*, Malden, MA, Blackwell Publishing, 2005, pp. 311-324.

Boedeker Jr., Edgar C., "Individual and Community in Early Heidegger: Situating Das Man, the Man-Self, and Self-Ownership in Dasein's Ontological Structure," in *Inquiry,* 44:1, 2001, pp. 63-99.

Brandom, Robert, "Heidegger's Categories," Dreyfus, Hubert L. and Wrathall, Mark A. (eds.), *A Companion to Heidegger*, Malden, MA, Blackwell Publishers, 2005, pp. 214-232.

Carman, Taylor, "On Being Social: A Reply to Olafson," in *Inquiry*, 37:2 (1994), pp. 203-223.

Crowell, Steven, "Subjectivity: Locating the First-Person in Being and Time," in *Inquiry*, 44:4 (2001), pp. 433-454.

Davis, Bret W., "Introduction: Key Concepts in Heidegger's Thinking of Being," Davis, Bret W. (ed.), *Martin Heidegger: Key Concepts*, Durham, UK, Acumen, 2010, pp. 1-16.

Descartes, Rene, *Meditations on First Philosophy*, Bennett, Jonathan (tr.), (April, 2007), http://www.earlymoderntexts.com/pdf/descmedi.pdf [Accessed 14 July 2013].

Dreyfus, Hubert L., *Being-in-the-World: A Commentary on Heidegger's* Being and Time*, Division I,* Cambridge, MA, MIT Press, 1991.

Dreyfus, Hubert L., "Interpreting Heidegger on Das Man." *Inquiry,* 38, 423-30.

Dreyfus, Hubert and Wrathall, Mark, "Martin Heidegger: An Introduction to His Thought, Work, and Life," Dreyfus, Hubert L. and Wrathall, Mark A. (eds.), *A Companion to Heidegger*, Malden, MA, Blackwell Publishing, 2005, pp. 1-15.

Gelvin, Michael, *A Commentary on Heidegger's* Being and Time*, Revised Edition,* DeKalb, IL, Northern Illinois University Press, 1989.

Guignon, Charles B. *Heidegger and the Problem of Knowledge*. Indianapolis: Hackett Publishing, 1983.

Guignon, Charles B. "Heidegger's Authenticity' Revisited." *The Review of Metaphysics* 38 (2):321 - 339. (1984).

Haugeland. John. "Heidegger on Being a Person." *Nous* 16 (1982): 15-26.

Haugeland, John, "Letting Be," Crowell, Steven and Malpas, Jeff (eds.), *Transcendental Heidegger*, Stanford, CA, Stanford University Press, 2007, pp. 93-103.

Haugeland, John. "Reading Brandom Reading Heidegger." *European Journal of Philosophy* 13 (3):421–428. (2005).

Heidegger, Martin. *Being and Time*. Macquarrie, John and Robinson, Edward (tr.), New York, Harper & Row, 1962.

Heidegger, Martin, *A History of the Concept of Time: Prolegomena*, Bloomington, IN, Indiana University Press, 2009.

James, William, "Pragmatism's Conception of Truth," Thayer, H.S. (ed.), *Pragmatism: The Classic Writings*, New York, Hackett Publishing, 1982.

Kant, Immanuel, *Critique of Pure Reason*, Smith, Norman Kemp (tr.), London, Macmillan, 1968.

Lefebvre, Henri, *Everyday Life in the Modern World*, Rabinovitch, Sacha (tr.), New York, Harper Torchbooks, 1971.

Lefebvre, Henri, *The Production of Space*, Nicholson-Smith, Donald (tr.), Oxford, UK, Blackwell Publishers, 1991.

Malpas, Jeff, *Heidegger and the Thinking of Place*, Cambridge, MA, MIT Press, 2012.

Malpas, Jeff, *Heidegger's Topology*, Cambridge, MA, MIT Press, 2006.

Mulhall, Stephen, *Routledge Philosophy Guidebook to Heidegger and* Being and Time, London, Routledge, 1996.

Okrent, Mark, "The 'I Think' and the For-the-Sake-of-Which," Crowell, Steven and Malpas, Jeff (eds.), *Transcendental Heidegger*, Stanford, CA, Stanford University Press, 2007.

Olafson, Frederick A., "Heidegger a'la Wittgenstein or 'Coping' with Professor Dreyfus," in *Inquiry*, 37:1 (1994), pp. 45-64.

Ortega, Mariana. "Exiled space, in-between space: existential spatiality in Ana Mendieta's *Siluetas Series*." Philosophy & Geography, vol. 7, no. 1, February 2004.

Polt, Richard, *Heidegger: An Introduction*, Ithaca, NY, Cornell University Press, 1999.

Sartre, Jean-Paul, *Being and Nothingness: An Essay on Phenomenological Ontology*, Barnes, Hazel E. (tr.), New York, Simon & Schuster, 1956.

Schatzki, Theodore R. "Early Heidegger on Sociality," Dreyfus, Hubert L. and Wrathall, Mark A. (eds.), *A Companion to Heidegger*, Malden, MA, Blackwell Publishing, 2005, pp. 233-247.

Schmid, Hans Bernhard, "The Broken We," in *Tonoc*, 2:11 (2005), pp. 16-27.

Stapleton, Timothy, "Dasein as Being in the World," Davis, Bret W. (ed.), *Martin Heidegger: Key Concepts,* Durham, UK, Acumen, 2010, pp. 44-56.

Taylor, Charles, "Engaged Agency and Background in Heidegger," Guignon, Charles B. (ed.), *The Cambridge Companion to Heidegger,* Cambridge, UK, Cambridge University Press, 1993, pp. 317-326.

Wittgenstein, Ludwig, *Tractatus Logico-Philosophicus,* Pears, D.F. and McGuinness, B.F. (tr.), London, Routledge and Kegan Paul, 1961.

Wrathall, Mark, *How to Read Heidegger*, New York, W.W. Norton, 2006.

Wrathall, Mark A., "Unconcealment," Dreyfus, Hubert L. and Wrathall, Mark A. (eds.), *A Companion to Heidegger*, Malden, MA, Blackwell Publishing, 2005, pp. 337-357.

www.ingramcontent.com/pod-product-compliance
Lightning Source LLC
Chambersburg PA
CBHW060521280326
41933CB00014B/3050